THE
CORNER
OFFICE

THE
CORNER
OFFICE

INDISPENSABLE AND
UNEXPECTED LESSONS
FROM CEOS ON HOW TO
LEAD AND SUCCEED

Adam Bryant

Times Books
Henry Holt and Company
New York

Times Books
Henry Holt and Company, LLC
Publishers since 1866
175 Fifth Avenue
New York, New York 10010

Henry Holt® is a registered trademark of Henry Holt and Company, LLC.

Library of Congress Cataloging-in-Publication Data

Bryant, Adam.
   The corner office : indispensable and unexpected lessons from CEOs on
how to lead and succeed / Adam Bryant.—1st ed.
      p. cm.
   Includes index.
   ISBN 978-0-8050-9306-3
   1. Leadership.   2. Executive ability.   3. Management.   4. Chief
executive officers.   I. Title.
   HD57.7.B784 2011
   658.4'092—dc22   2010042970

Henry Holt books are available for special promotions and premiums.
For details contact: Director, Special Markets.

Designed by Meryl Sussman Levavi

Printed in the United States of America
10   9   8   7

To Jeanetta, Anna, and Sophia

CONTENTS

Part Two MANAGING

Part Three LEADING

LIST OF INTERVIEWS

Daniel P. Amos, CEO, Aflac

Richard Anderson, CEO, Delta Air Lines

Steven A. Ballmer, CEO, Microsoft

George S. Barrett, CEO, Cardinal Health

Carol Bartz, CEO, Yahoo

Gordon M. Bethune, former CEO, Continental Airlines

Greg Brenneman, chairman, CCMP Capital

Bobbi Brown, founder, Bobbi Brown Cosmetics

Tim Brown, CEO, IDEO

Ursula M. Burns, CEO, Xerox

Bill Carter, partner and co-founder, Fuse

Eduardo Castro-Wright, vice chairman, Wal-Mart Stores

John T. Chambers, CEO, Cisco Systems

Cristóbal Conde, CEO, SunGard

Andrew Cosslett, CEO, InterContinental Hotels Group

Susan Docherty, vice president, General Motors

John Donahoe, CEO, eBay

Brian Dunn, CEO, Best Buy

Deborah Dunsire, CEO, Millennium

Jana Eggers, CEO, Spreadshirt

Drew Gilpin Faust, president, Harvard University

William D. Green, CEO, Accenture

Mindy Grossman, CEO, HSN

Omar Hamoui, founder and CEO, AdMob

Steve Hannah, CEO, The Onion

Linda Heasley, CEO, The Limited

Tony Hsieh, CEO, Zappos

Jen-Hsun Huang, CEO, Nvidia

Linda Hudson, CEO, BAE Systems

Robert Iger, CEO, Disney

Judith Jamison, artistic director, Alvin Ailey American Dance Theater

Jeffrey Katzenberg, CEO, DreamWorks Animation

Guy Kawasaki, co-founder, Alltop, and managing director, Garage Technology Ventures

Lawrence W. Kellner, CEO, Continental Airlines

Wendy Kopp, founder and CEO, Teach for America

Jacqueline Kosecoff, CEO, Prescription Solutions

Barbara J. Krumsiek, CEO, Calvert Group

Debra L. Lee, CEO, BET Networks

Niki Leondakis, chief operating officer, Kimpton Hotels and
Restaurants

Dawn Lepore, CEO, Drugstore.com

Dany Levy, founder, DailyCandy.com

Terry J. Lundgren, CEO, Macy's

Susan Lyne, CEO, Gilt Groupe

Sheila Lirio Marcelo, CEO, Care.com

Michael Mathieu, CEO, YuMe

Gary E. McCullough, CEO, Career Education Corporation

Nancy McKinstry, CEO, Walters Kluwer

Nell Minow, co-founder, The Corporate Library

Meridee A. Moore, founder, Watershed Asset Management

Alan R. Mulally, CEO, Ford Motor Company

Anne Mulcahy, former CEO, Xerox

Sharon Napier, CEO, Partners + Napier

Shantanu Narayen, CEO, Adobe Systems

Vineet Nayar, CEO, HCL Technologies

David C. Novak, CEO, Yum Brands

Clarence Otis Jr., CEO, Darden Restaurants

Mark Pincus, CEO, Zynga

Joseph J. Plumeri, CEO, Willis Group Holdings

Lisa Price, founder, Carol's Daughter

Quintin E. Primo III, co-founder and CEO, Capri Capital
Partners

James E. Rogers, CEO, Duke Energy

Kasper Rorsted, CEO, Henkel

Dan Rosensweig, CEO, Chegg

Stephen I. Sadove, CEO, Saks

James J. Schiro, CEO, Zurich Financial Services

Robert W. Selander, CEO, MasterCard

Kevin Sharer, CEO, Amgen

Carol Smith, senior vice president and chief brand officer, Elle Group

Jilly Stephens, executive director, City Harvest

Jeffrey Swartz, CEO, Timberland

Teresa A. Taylor, chief operating officer, Qwest Communications

Kip Tindell, CEO, The Container Store

Will Wright, videogame developer

Tachi Yamada, president, Global Health Program, Bill and Melinda Gates Foundation

AUTHOR'S NOTE

The material in this book is derived from the author's interviews with more than seventy CEOs and other top executives at large companies, small companies, nonprofit organizations, and educational and artistic institutions. The executives' responses were recorded, transcribed, and condensed for publication. Their job titles reflect the status of the executives at the time they were interviewed. The conversations occurred between March 2009 and July 2010.

THE CORNER OFFICE

INTRODUCTION

For investors and business journalists, stock-price fluctuations and quarterly results offer a steady stream of report cards for evaluating a CEO's work. And then, every spring, when proxy season rolls around and companies disclose the compensation packages for top executives, another round of report cards begins. This transparency keeps people honest and creates a relatively level playing field (except, of course, when the numbers lie). From these data, a story line emerges around the CEOs as strategists, and we focus on their successes, their failures, their challenges. Have they sized up the industry landscape correctly and developed a plan to beat their competitors? Are they executing this plan in a disciplined fashion?

For this book, I was interested in pursuing a different story line about CEOs—their own personal stories, free of numbers, theories, jargon, charts, and with minimal discussions of their companies or industries. I wanted to hear what they had learned from their ups and downs, their stories about how they learned to lead, the mistakes they made along the way, how they fostered supportive corporate cultures, and how they do the same things that every other manager does—interview job candidates, run meetings, promote teamwork, manage their time, and give and get feedback.

While setting overall business strategy is certainly an important part of a CEO's job, leadership shapes every part of their day. Once they have a plan, the challenge becomes making sure they have the right people on the team, and getting the most out of them and the broader organization. CEOs may not study leadership in books or develop new silver-bullet theories, but they are experts in leadership because they practice it daily. And many of them have spent the better part of a decade or more honing their leadership styles, through trial and error, studying what works and what doesn't, and then mentoring others.

CEOs have learned firsthand what it takes to succeed and rise to the top of an organization. From the corner office, they can watch others attempt a similar climb, and notice the qualities that set people apart. As they evaluate talent, they learn to divine why one person is more likely to succeed than another. When they bring in talent from the outside, they watch as some new hires blend in better than others. Who succeeds? Who fails? Why? It's a feedback loop that expands with every additional person they manage, creating a kind of laboratory for studying the qualities that enable people to succeed. CEOs study team dynamics, too. If one division or group consistently outperforms another, why is that? What leadership skills does that division or group leader possess? Finally, there is feedback from the marketplace. In business, there are constant judgments and scores. From quarter to quarter, CEOs can determine whether their strategies and leadership styles are working, and whether they need to be adjusted.

CEOs face criticism from many corners, and it is often deserved. But there is no arguing that they have achieved a great deal, through a combination of smarts, hard work, attitude, and commitment. They have much to offer beyond a return on a shareholder's investment.

∽

I have spent much of my two decades in business journalism interviewing CEOs and asking variations of the question "What's the strategy for your company?" But I found myself growing more interested in asking them questions like "How do you do what you do?" "How did you learn to do what you do?" and "What lessons have you learned that you can share with others?"

I developed an appreciation for what effective leadership can mean for a company—and the skills a CEO brings to the table— when I covered the airline industry in the mid-1990s as a reporter for the *New York Times*. It was a particularly turbulent time in the business, and some of the executives running the carriers were larger-than-life characters. The airline industry, I realized, was like the National Football League. There are team colors and logos— and people have strong passions about which teams they love and hate. Each team has roughly the same equipment, and, as in football, the playing field is reasonably level. One airline can instantly copy an effective strategy from a competitor, whether it's a fare sale or a new twist to the frequent-flyer program. Like defensive and offensive players in football, the employees of each airline are organized into their own specialized units—pilots, flight attendants, mechanics, baggage handlers, gate agents, white-collar workers. I found that what really made the difference from one airline to another was leadership. The culture and tone started at the top, and each company reflected the personalities of its CEO, whether it was Robert L. Crandall at American, Herb Kelleher at Southwest, Stephen M. Wolf at United, or Gordon M. Bethune at Continental. The leader who understood how to get his employees to work together as a team had an advantage.

Gordon Bethune in particular faced a difficult challenge in 1994 when he took over Continental, which had made trips through bankruptcy court and had become a punch line for airline jokes on late-night television.

He figured out a simple plan about what mattered to customers, and promised to share rewards with the entire workforce if they hit certain performance measures better than their competitors. He believed that the additional revenue from pulling away premium customers from Continental's competitors and the reduced costs from a better on-time record would more than justify the cost of paying out some of the benefits to workers.

"What you measure is what gets accomplished," Bethune told me during one of several conversations we had in the mid-1990s. "Most businesses fail because they want the right things but measure the wrong things, and they get the wrong results."

Bethune was fast on his feet with expressions that crystallized a problem or question. He didn't apologize, for example, for bringing in high-priced talent from the outside to join his management team. "Now you can hire a brain surgeon, or you can hire a proctologist at half-price who wants to learn," he said. He invested in better service and employee morale instead of single-mindedly cutting costs. "You can make a pizza so cheap, nobody will buy it," he was fond of saying.

He understood that basic ideas were reliable tools, and his turnaround success at Continental brought credibility to his keep-it-simple approach. No jargon, no theories. Just memorable insights and stories from a CEO that had the ring of truth.

"If you say three things in a row that make sense, people will vote for you," he said.

And one good story about leadership and management from an executive who has worked hard to learn it is equal to ten theories about what should be or could be done in a certain situation.

~

I discovered over the course of in-depth interviews with more than seventy CEOs and other high-ranking executives that they all have remarkable stories to tell, filled with insights and lessons for others. I've studied the transcripts for patterns and connections, and organized them into the chapters that make up the three parts of this book: "Succeeding," "Managing," and "Leading."

My goal is not only to offer a new story line about CEOs as managers but also to provide some back-to-basics help for managers at all levels of business, particularly since so many of the grand notions about transformative business practices have failed to live up to their billing amid the rubble of the busted economy. Employees have higher expectations of their employers now, too, and the companies that can engage them deeply will win the battle for talent.

To be sure, not all CEOs are successes, and a falling stock price can be a sign of an executive out of his depth rather than a lesson in adversity that will make the CEO, and his company, stronger in the long run.

But after interviewing dozens of executives, I was reminded of the first line of Leo Tolstoy's *Anna Karenina*: "All happy families are alike; each unhappy family is unhappy in its own way." Many of the CEOs I interviewed resembled one another in their approach. They listen, learn, assess what's working, what's not and why, and then make adjustments. They are quick studies, and they also tend to be good teachers, because they understand the process of learning and

can explain what they've learned to others. They seem eager to discuss their hard-earned insights rather than hold on to them as if
they were proprietary software.

They shared many of the same notions about leadership and
management. They put a premium on direct and frank communication, and flattening the organization. They try to use questions
more than statements, so that their employees take ownership of
their roles rather than simply take orders from the CEO. They
provide a sharp contrast to command-and-control leadership styles
of the past, when CEOs isolated themselves from employees—
literally, in some cases, with a private elevator down to a reserved
parking space, and in more subtle ways. Now they want to mix it
up. "I love that people push back on me, and it gets to better ideas,"
said Sheila Lirio Marcelo, CEO of Care.com. "I'm really focused
on pushing people to gain the confidence to logically debate with a
CEO."

Many successful CEOs reward honesty and input, and show
their interest in learning what others think, by holding town-hall
meetings, seeking the advice of people at all levels of the company,
and asking employees what they would do if they were in charge.
"The best ideas or important ideas or new ideas can come from
anywhere in an organization," said Tim Brown, the CEO of the
design consulting firm IDEO, recalling how a boss valued his
opinions when Brown was in his early twenties. "So you'd better do
a good job of spotting and promoting them when they come, and
not let people's positions dictate how influential their ideas are."

These CEOs also try to create a culture of learning in their
organizations, so that, collectively, employees can adjust to the constant changes and challenges of business. The global business environment requires collaborative learning. No single person has the
answer anymore, and smart companies try to harness the multi-

plier effect of bringing people together to share their unique experiences and perspectives on a problem.

"I like building teams with people who come from very different backgrounds and have very different experiences," said Susan Docherty, a vice president of General Motors. "I don't just mean diverse teams, in terms of men and women or people of different color or origin. I like people who have worked in different places in the world than I have, because they bring a lot more context to the discussion. That's something that I value a tremendous amount. I make sure that when I'm looking at people for my team, it's not just what's on their résumé—their strengths or weaknesses or what they've accomplished—but it's the way they think. I can learn twice as much, twice as quickly, if I've got people who think differently than I do around the table."

This book is meant to be that metaphorical table, at which dozens of CEOs, from vastly different backgrounds, countries, and industries, share their insights on how they lead and manage and the best lessons they've learned. These executives don't live up to their own ideals every day—nobody does—and at times some of them have fallen well short. But that doesn't diminish the value of their specific insights or the benefits from hearing them discuss their goals for their companies, and for themselves as leaders. The conversations that inform this book are a kind of time-out from the weekly churn of business—earnings, strategy statements, PowerPoint presentations, SEC filings—and are designed instead to reveal more about CEOs as people, not just as the faces of their companies.

In the chapters that follow, I have tried to play the role of dinner-party host, encouraging lively discussion and pointing out connections among the people gathered. My goal is to frame the conversations but not to dominate them, and to let the people around the table share their stories in their own voices. It's not just what they say that's important—how they say it is revealing, too.

Everybody will read this book differently. Some passages will resonate more than others, and some readers will connect more closely with the experiences and insights of certain executives. That's the nature of collaborative learning. There is no single way to lead or to manage. We all have to figure out what makes sense on our own, and develop our own story lines as leaders. The insights offered by the CEOs in these pages can help speed the learning process for those coming after them and offer fresh approaches to peers looking for new ideas. It doesn't have to be so lonely at the top, or during the climb along the way.

PART ONE

SUCCEEDING

1.

PASSIONATE CURIOSITY

Imagine one hundred people working in a large company. They're roughly the same age, around thirty-five. They're all vice presidents and share many of the same qualities that got them where they are. They're smart, collegial, and hardworking. They consider themselves team players. They have positive attitudes and they're good communicators. They're conscientious about their jobs. They have integrity.

If everyone shares these qualities, what is going to determine who gets the next promotion? Who is going to move up not just one level, but the one after that, and the one after that? As they move up near the peak of their companies and the ranks thin out, the competition for the top spots is even tougher. Who will land the jobs that report directly to the CEO? What will set them apart from the crowd? When it's time for the CEO to move on, who will get the nod from the board to move into the corner office?

In other words, what does it take to lead an organization—whether it's an athletic team, a nonprofit, a start-up, or a multinational corporation? What, at the end of the day, are the keys, the x-factors, to achieving the highest levels of success?

Interviews with CEOs and other leading executives point to five essentials for success—qualities that most of the CEOs share, and which they look for in others when they hire.

The good news: these keys to success are not genetic. It's not as if you have to be tall or left-handed. You don't have to be born into the kind of family that has you swinging a golf club or playing chess not long after you're out of diapers. These qualities are developed through attitude, habit, and discipline—factors that are within everyone's control. They will make you stand out in any setting or organization. They will make you a better employee, manager, and leader. They will lift the trajectory of your career and speed your progress along it.

The qualities these executives share: Passionate curiosity. Battle-hardened confidence. Team smarts. A simple mindset. Fearlessness.

These aren't theories. They come from decades of collective experience of top executives who have shared their perspectives and stories about their own rise through the ranks, and why they promote some executives over others in their organizations. Each of these qualities is important and multifaceted enough to have a chapter of its own, starting with passionate curiosity.

~

Many successful CEOs are passionately curious people.

It is a side of them rarely seen in the media and in investor meetings, and there is a reason for that. In business, CEOs are supposed to project calm confidence and breezy authority as they take an audience through presentations filled with charts predicting steady gains in revenue and profit. Certainty is the game face they wear. They are paid to have answers, to see around corners, and to have a firm grasp of the competitive landscape. When they are right, their pictures appear on the covers of glossy business magazines. The message is, they've got it figured out. They've cracked the code.

But get them away from these familiar scripts and settings and ask them instead about important lessons they've learned over the course of their lives, how they lead and manage day-to-day, and a different side emerges. They wrestle with tough issues. They share stories about failures and doubts and mistakes. They ask big-picture questions. They seem like eager students who devour insights and lessons, and are genuinely, enthusiastically interested in everything going on around them. Take them away from balance sheets and strategy and they seem more like natural teachers with agile minds. They wonder why things work the way they do and whether those things can be improved upon. They want to know people's stories, and what they do.

It's this relentless questioning that leads entrepreneurs to spot new opportunities and helps managers understand the people who work for them, and how to get them to work together effectively. It is no coincidence that more than one executive uttered the same phrase when describing what, ultimately, is the CEO's job: "I am a student of human nature."

The same mental agility enables a CEO to engage with every one of his or her direct reports—in marketing, finance, operations, R&D—and be able to grasp the key issues, without the specialized experience of each of their subordinates. The CEOs are not necessarily the smartest people in the room, but they are the best students—the letters could just as easily stand for Chief Education Officer. They learn, they teach, and they understand people and the business world, and then bring all that knowledge together to drive their organizations forward.

"You learn from everybody," said Alan R. Mulally, the CEO of the Ford Motor Company. "I've always just wanted to learn everything, to understand anybody that I was around—why they thought what they did, why they did what they did, what worked for them, what didn't work."

Dawn Lepore, the CEO of Drugstore.com, took advantage of her role as the chief technology officer at Schwab to learn from other CEOs about leadership.

"I had the benefit of being able to interact with a lot of technology CEOs, because they would come to sell to me," Lepore said. "So I got to meet with Scott McNealy, Bill Gates, Steve Ballmer, John Chambers, and others. And I would always say to them, 'Let's talk about your product, but I'd really love to hear more about your company, your culture, your leadership.' So I really picked their brains. I learned something from every single one of them. And I've served on a bunch of different boards, and I've had an opportunity to just learn from the CEO of the company as well as all the other board members."

Some people consider themselves more left-brained, analytical thinkers, while others see themselves as more creative, right-brained types. But not these executives. Nothing is ruled out. Everything can be important and interesting, a new area to be studied and grasped.

"I'm not a high numbers person and I'm not a high emotional person," said Carol Smith, senior vice president and chief brand officer for the Elle Group, which publishes *Elle* magazine. "I'm a total combination of the two. I definitely have a middle brain, which I think might be a very nice brain to have in this position. I think it's served me well."

David C. Novak, the CEO of Yum Brands, which operates fast-food chains like Pizza Hut, Taco Bell, and KFC, likes to hire people who have this balance.

"In the best of all worlds," Novak said, "you want someone who's whole-brained—someone who is analytical and can also be creative enough to come up with the ideas and galvanize the organization around a direction that's going to take us to someplace that we might not have known we could go to. I think it's easier to find left-brained people than it is to find truly creative people. I think what we need in our leaders, the people who ultimately run our companies and run our functions, is whole-brained people—people who can be analytical but also have that creativity, the right-brain side of the equation. There's more and more of a premium on that today than ever before."

Jen-Hsun Huang, the CEO of Nvidia, the computer graphics company, said both sides of his brain play important roles in finding new opportunities.

"I don't like making decisions with analytics," he said. "I actually like making decisions with intuition. I like to validate the decision with analytics. I don't believe you can analyze your way into success. I think it's too complicated. You have to use intuition, which is everything—your artistic sensibility, your intellectual sensibility, experience. Now once you pick a direction, you want to try to validate it as often as you can. I think successful people have wonderful capabilities with both."

❧

Why "passionate curiosity"? The phrase is more than the sum of its parts. Many CEOs will cite passion or curiosity as an important trait in the people they look to hire.

They make persuasive cases for why each is important.

"What I really want to know is what kind of person I'm dealing with," said Joseph J. Plumeri, the CEO of Willis Group Holdings, an insurance broker. "So I only ask one question. I say, 'Tell me what you're passionate about.' That's it. Whatever you want to talk about. Tell me what you're passionate about. Digging holes. Riding bikes. I'm looking to see if they've got a passion. I'm looking to see if there's anything inside, other than what they do. And how passionate could they be, therefore, about being here? And how excited and involved could they be? I'm not looking for a mirror image of me. I'm just looking for somebody who gets turned on about something. If you find that kind of person, then these are the people you want to climb hills with and climb mountains with."

Robert Iger, the CEO of Disney, said curiosity was a key quality he looked for in job candidates.

"I love curiosity, particularly in our business—being curious about the world, but also being curious about your business, new business models, new technology," he said. "If you're not curious about technology and its potential impact on your life, then you'll have no clue what its impact might be on someone else's life."

Passion. Curiosity. Both are important. But those words, separately, fall short of capturing the quality that sets these CEOs apart. There are plenty of people who are passionate, but many of their passions are focused on just one area. There are a lot of curious people in the world, but they can also be wallflowers.

But "passionate curiosity"—a phrase used by Nell Minow, the co-founder of The Corporate Library—is a better description of the quality that helps set CEOs apart: an infectious sense of fascination with everything around them.

Passionate curiosity, Minow said, "is indispensable, no matter what the job is. You want somebody who is just alert and very awake and engaged with the world and wanting to know more."

People with this quality are sponges for information, for insights, wherever they are, whatever they're doing.

"I think that the best leaders are really pattern thinkers," said David Novak of Yum Brands. "They want to get better. Are they continually trying to better themselves? Are they looking outside for ideas that will help them grow the business? I look at it in the context of their own personal development. They're constantly trying to learn how they can become better leaders and they're constantly trying to learn how they can build a better business. They soak up everything they can possibly soak up so that they can become the best possible leaders they can be. And then they share that with others."

◡

Though CEOs are paid to have answers, their greatest contribution to their organizations may be asking the right questions—a skill that starts with passionate curiosity.

They recognize that they can't have the answer to everything—that's why they hire specialists to handle different parts of their organization—but they can push their company in the right direction and marshal the collective energy of their employees by asking the right questions. That, after all, is where the new opportunities are.

"In business, the big prizes are found when you can ask a question that challenges the corporate orthodoxy that exists in every business," said Andrew Cosslett, the CEO of InterContinental Hotels Group. "In every business I've worked in, there's been a lot of cost and value locked up in things that are deemed to be 'the way we do things around here,' or they're deemed to be critical to—in the hotel world—a guest experience. So you have to talk to people and ask questions. I just keep asking people, 'Why do you do that?'"

It's an important lesson. For all the furrowed-brow seriousness and certainty that you often encounter in the business world, some of the most important advances come from asking, much like a persistent five-year-old, the simplest questions. Why do you do that? How come it's done this way? Is there a better way?

"I do think that's something we forget," said Tim Brown, the CEO of IDEO, the design consulting firm. "As leaders, probably the most important role we can play is asking the right questions. But the bit we forget is that it is, in itself, a creative process. Those right questions aren't just kind of lying around on the ground to be picked up and asked. When I go back and look at the great leaders—Roosevelt, Churchill—one of the things that occur to me is they somehow had the ability to frame the question in a way that nobody else would have thought about. In design, that's everything, right? If you don't ask the right questions, then you're never going to get the right solution. I spent too much of my career feeling like I'd done a really good job answering the wrong question. And that was because I was letting other people give me the question. One of the things that I've tried to do more and more—and I obviously have the opportunity to do as a leader—is to take ownership of the question. And so I'm much more interested these days in having debates about what the questions should be than I necessarily am about the solutions."

Jen-Hsun Huang of Nvidia said that his leadership style today is defined by questions rather than answers.

"It's not possible for the CEO to know everything, but it is possible for us to add value to literally everything," Huang said. "And the reason for that is, if you're the CEO, you're probably better at looking around corners than most. You probably have better intuition than most. You're probably able to see the forest better than most. You're probably able to deal with complexity better than most. And so you bring a perspective that is unique. By asking the right questions, you can get to the heart of the issue right away. It's almost possible now for me to go through a day and do nothing but ask questions and have my sensibility, my perspective and what's important to me be perfectly clear to everybody without making a statement at all."

Asking questions. Showing genuine enthusiasm. Being interested in the world. It sounds so simple, yet not everyone displays those qualities, particularly in a business culture that values jut-jawed certainty. Top executives who are passionately curious can also spot like-minded people from a mile away. They will pick them out of a crowd, and even hire them on the spot—another sign of how rare this quality is.

"I once hired somebody who wasn't looking for a job," said Nell Minow of The Corporate Library. "A guy called to ask me some questions about some corporate governance issue and I just thought he was so bright. I said, 'I'll put some materials together for you and put them in the mail.' And he said, 'Can I come over and pick them up right now?' I said, 'Are you looking for a job?' And he said, 'Well, I'm in an internship right now. I just graduated from college and my internship is going to finish up at the end of the summer.' I told him, 'If you are looking for a job when the internship ends, I'm going to hire you.' And I did."

James J. Schiro, CEO of Zurich Financial Services, said he sometimes picked assistants—to travel with him and help him get things done—just by keeping his eye out for young people who are "smart, bright, energetic."

"The person who works with me now I met on a road show," Schiro said. "He was one of the bankers, and I said, 'I'd like to talk to him.' He came in, and I said, 'Philippe, how would you like to work for me?' He said, 'Doing what?' I said, 'I don't know. I've watched you. You understand this industry. You know more about this industry than I do, and you can just work for me for a year, and then after that year, somebody in this organization will hire you.'"

Some CEOs worked early on as an assistant—a right-hand man or woman—to a top executive. Did they then ultimately rise to top jobs because of that early experience as an assistant, seeing the world through a CEO's eyes at a young age? Or were they chosen for those assistant jobs because top executives had a keen eye for people who displayed passionate curiosity? Undoubtedly both are true.

The early career of Ursula M. Burns, the CEO of Xerox, is a case in point. She was noticed by top executives early on, and promoted to a level in the organization that few get to see at a young age.

The sharp inflection point in her career at Xerox came in 1989, when she was working in product development and planning. She was invited to a work-life discussion. Diversity initiatives came up, and somebody asked whether such initiatives lowered hiring standards. Wayland Hicks, a senior Xerox executive running the meeting, patiently explained that that was not true.

"I was stunned," Burns said. "I actually told him, 'I was surprised that you gave this assertion any credence.'"

After that meeting, she revisited the issue with Hicks, and a few weeks later he asked her to meet with him in his office. She figured that she was about to be reprimanded or fired. Instead, Hicks told her she had been right to be concerned but also wrong for handling it so forcefully. Then he told her he wanted to meet regularly with her.

"She was enormously curious," Hicks explained. "She wanted to know why we were doing some things at the time, and she was always prepared in a way that I thought was very refreshing." He offered her a job as his executive assistant in January 1990, when she was thirty-one. She would travel with Hicks, sit in on important meetings, and help him get things done. She accepted, and they talked a lot about leadership during downtime.

Burns continued to speak her mind and ask questions inside Xerox—particularly on an occasion in mid-1991 when the stakes were unusually high. At the time, Paul A. Allaire, Xerox's president, held monthly meetings with top managers, and Burns and other assistants were invited to sit in, but off to the side.

Burns noticed a pattern. Allaire would announce, "We have to stop hiring." But then the company would hire a thousand people. The next month, same thing. So she raised her hand. "I'm a little confused, Mr. Allaire," she said. "If you keep saying, 'No hiring,' and we hire a thousand people every month, who can say 'No hiring' and make it actually happen?" She remembers that he stared at her with a "Why did you ask that question?" look and then the meeting moved on.

Later, the phone rang. Allaire wanted to see her in his office. She figured that it was not good news. But Allaire wanted to poach her from Hicks, so she could be his executive assistant. They, too, talked often about leadership. Allaire didn't want to discourage her candor but, like Hicks, he offered tips about how to be more effective—"like giving people credit for ideas that they didn't have but you sold to them, to give them ownership," Allaire recalled advising her. Allaire saw in her the right mix of energy, confidence, and curiosity—an eagerness to learn.

Burns was forceful about asking questions on her way to the corner office. "You have to learn and you have to be curious," her mother always told her.

And how does Burns describe her role today as CEO?

"The job is exactly not about having the right answers," she said. "The job is having great questions asked and great people helping you answer them. Not all the right questions come from you, either. But I have a perspective and a purview that allow me to have a different set of questions. If somebody comes to me with a problem, almost surely I'll send it back and say, 'Think about this. How about this? How about that?'"

As these CEOs have shown, asking good questions can help at every stage of a career, for people just starting out and for those in charge of an international corporation. It bears repeating. They show interest and enthusiasm, and they ask questions. They focus on being interested rather than trying to be interesting, as the saying goes. People who show this kind of initiative will find that it leads to important relationships—at work and outside of work. That's how people find mentors, and how they connect with leaders of the company.

Some people in business refer to the 80/20 rule, a variation of a concept called the Pareto Principle. It refers to the idea that 20 percent of the people in any company do 80 percent of the work. Now, think again about those one hundred people in an organization, all at the same rank. If twenty of them are going to be the workhorses of the group, there will be an even smaller number who go beyond their assigned tasks, and take an interest in the people and the organization outside their job descriptions. They will stand out.

Show some passionate curiosity—it is a simple rule with an enormous payoff.

"If you give positive vibes, if you show an interest, by and large a lot of people will react," said Stephen I. Sadove, the CEO of Saks. "Not everybody, but people tend to react. When people show an interest in reaching out, I tend to react to them."

2.

BATTLE-HARDENED CONFIDENCE

Consider those one hundred employees again—all vice presidents at the same company. As their bosses size up this group, some qualities are easier to spot than others. Passionate curiosity? It's there for all to see. There's an energy, a buzz, from people who have it, and you can pick them out of a crowd.

Other qualities are tougher to discern, especially the ability to handle adversity. Everybody faces challenges of some kind or another in their life, but some people deal with adversity better than others. And then there are those who embrace it, who relish it, who want the tough assignment when the pressure is on. These people have plowed through tough circumstances, and they know what they're capable of handling. They have a track record of overcoming adversity, of failing and getting up off the mat to get the job done, no matter what. They have battle-hardened confidence.

The same is true for companies. Many CEOs say their corporate culture has been strengthened in painful periods when nothing seemed to be working, and the leadership had to pull everyone together to establish their core values and beliefs.

If there were some test to find out whether a person had this quality, it would be a huge moneymaker. But people, and companies, reveal how they deal with adversity only in the context of new challenges—when they are faced with potential or real failure and the status quo is not an option. The best predictor of behavior is past performance, and that's why so many CEOs interview job candidates about how they dealt with failure in the past. They want to know if somebody is the kind of person who takes ownership of challenges, or starts looking for excuses because there are too many factors beyond their control.

People can talk a good game in job interviews, but that talk can seem meaningless when someone is confronted with a difficult task and the moment of truth arrives. In such circumstances, some people fold.

"I think hiring great people remains extremely, extremely hard," said Jen-Hsun Huang of Nvidia. "The reason for that is this: It all comes down to how somebody deals with adversity. You can never really tell how somebody deals with adversity, whether it's adversity that's created by the environment or adversity that you're creating for them. As the CEO, as a leader, sometimes you have to put people in the hot seat—not because you want them to be in a hot seat, but because the hot seat needs to have somebody sitting on it. And so you need a great player on it. When you have a difficult situation and you need somebody to take it and run with it, some people just take it and make it happen. They feed on adversity. There are some people who, in the face of adversity, become more calm. When the world is falling apart, I actually think my heart rate goes down. I find that I think best when I'm under adversity. Some people see adversity and they just cower, as talented as they are. You could ask them about the adversity they had in the past, but you never really know the intensity of that adversity."

∾

Many CEOs seem driven by a strong work ethic forged in adversity. Perhaps they started working at a young age and always had jobs as they grew up. Others worked because they had little choice, because they grew up in homes where money was tight. As they moved up in organizations, the responsibilities grew in scale, but the attitude remained the same—this is my job, and I'm going to take care of it, and own it. Because of that attitude, they are rewarded with more responsibilities, challenges, and promotions.

"I grew up dirt poor," said Carol Bartz, the CEO of Yahoo. "My mom died when I was eight, so my grandmother raised my brother and me. She had a great sense of humor, and she never really let things get to her. My favorite story is when we were on a farm in Wisconsin; I would have probably been thirteen. There was a snake up in the rafter of the machine shed. And we ran and said, 'Grandma, there's a snake.' And she came out and she knocked it down with a shovel, chopped its head off, and said, 'You could have done that.' And, you know, that's the tone she set. Just get it done. Just do it. Pick yourself up. Move on."

Nancy McKinstry, the CEO of Wolters Kluwer, the Dutch publishing and information company, also grew up in modest circumstances and learned to deal with the challenges of juggling schoolwork and jobs.

"I grew up without a lot of money," McKinstry said. "My mother was a schoolteacher and my parents were divorced when I was fairly young. So I watched my mother support a family on a schoolteacher's salary, which wasn't very much back in those days, and I watched her persevere. What I learned from her is the value of education and that hard work can make a difference. Because we didn't have a lot of money, I worked all the time. So when I was in college I worked two or three different jobs to fund my way through. So that ability to keep a lot of balls in the air and keep adapting to situations to try and make things happen every day was something that stuck with me."

When she's hiring, she looks for this quality in others. They don't necessarily need to have grown up in a household where money was tight. She's just looking for evidence that they handled difficult challenges.

"I like hiring people who have overcome adversity, because I believe I've seen in my own career that perseverance is really important," McKinstry said. "And if you can overcome some obstacle and keep moving up the field, it's tremendous. In any business you're going to be confronted with challenges, and so how you overcome them becomes important to your ability to drive the results forward. So when I interview folks, I will ask them directly: 'Give me an example of some adverse situation you faced, and what did you do about it, and what did you learn from it?' The people I've hired who have had that ability to describe the situation have always worked out, because they're able to sort of fall down, dust themselves off, and keep fighting the next day."

The CEOs' stories help bring to life a concept in psychology known as "locus of control." In general, it refers to a person's outlook and belief about what leads to success and failure in their life. Do they tend to blame failures on factors they cannot control, or do they believe they have the ability to shape events and circumstances by making the most of what they can control? In other words, do they make the most of whatever hand they are dealt? It's not just a sunny attitude. It's a positive attitude mixed with a sense of purpose and determination.

Ursula Burns of Xerox grew up poor on the Lower East Side of Manhattan, watching her mother struggle to raise her and her brother and sister, controlling what she could about their circumstances. Burns embodies this quality herself—making the most of those things she can control—and she wants her employees to embody them, too.

Burns's mother made ends meet by looking after other children. She also ironed shirts for a doctor who lived down the street and cleaned his office, bartering for things like medicine and even cleaning supplies. Burns's mother had many sayings—and she repeated them, often in blunt terms, over and over. "Where you are is not who you are," she would tell her children. "Don't act like you're from the gutter because you live in a place that's really close to the gutter."

She set firm expectations, Burns recalled. "She was very, very black-and-white and very clear about what responsibilities we had. One was that we had to be good people. And the second thing was that we had to be successful. And so her words for success were, 'You have to give'—and she would say this all the time—'more than you take away from the world.'"

Her mother, who died before she could see her daughter rise to the top at Xerox, also insisted that her children get a college education. "You have to worry about the things you can control," she would say. "Don't become a victim."

It was a theme that Burns herself touched on in a big meeting with Xerox employees not long after she took over as CEO. The lousy economy, the past boardroom dramas at Xerox—it was time to move on. She repeated one of her mother's sayings to a gathering of hundreds of sales reps: "Stuff happens to you, and then there's stuff that you happen to." Grammarians might take issue with the phrasing, but the message is clear. Don't let circumstances or potential excuses get the better of you. Stare them down, and make things happen.

Andrew Cosslett of InterContinental Hotels Group offered another example of how this quality is shared by people at the top. Cosslett had a rough childhood, and grew up living largely on his own from the time he was about sixteen. His schoolwork suffered as he focused more on rugby and other sports, and being "the boy about town," he said. He managed to scrape by in school through his teenage years, and grew more focused in his twenties.

Not long after he was named CEO, Cosslett was sitting with his top executives at an off-site meeting, and they went around the room, sharing stories about their backgrounds.

"It was a facilitated conversation as part of our time together, to try to understand what drove us, and our kind of purpose and meaning, what led us to be the people we are," Cosslett said. "What was extraordinary was that of the ten people in the room, nine of them had had very challenging teenage years, either with broken homes, family divorces, alcoholic parents, mothers getting beaten up, brothers or sisters dying. So 90 percent of the people in that room had something like that in their background. And I don't think that would be typical if you looked at the normal flow of society as a cross section. So there's something about what happened to them as kids that sort of pushed them on. And I think it's this thing about learning about your own strength that makes you mature more quickly and allows you to progress faster."

He elaborated on this quality, and discussed how he tries to learn in interviews whether a job candidate has it.

"You learn a lot very quickly about managing in difficult situations," he said. "One of the things that makes you see the world differently and forms you as an individual is if you've had to rely on your own wit and resources. If you've had a challenging upbringing, I think that's part of it. I think rugby is another one because there's no hiding place. It's a physical confrontation, and there's a moment of truth where you're going to be tested in a game. Everybody sees you, even though it's being done at high speed, and everybody knows whether you're the type to back down or stand up. It's never talked about, but everybody knows. And more than anything you know whether you're that type or the other type.

"If I'm recruiting people for very senior positions, I will delve quite extensively into their personal lives. I will look into how many times in their life they've been seriously tested emotionally, physically—where they've had to stand on their own feet and deal with something that they couldn't be prepared for. That could be in the business context. It could be in the family context, social context. And the ones who are the best, I've found, are the people who have had to confront something very difficult, and they're the people you can rely on when the going gets really tough because they've been there, and they know what they can do."

∾

For some companies and organizations, this quality is so important that they build their hiring process around it.

Every year, Teach for America sends its new recruits into often difficult school and classroom situations. The organization, founded in 1990 by Wendy Kopp, has learned how to screen for people who are likely to succeed in settings where the odds are stacked against them.

"We've done a lot of research to look at the personal characteristics that differentiate the people among our teachers who are the most successful," said Kopp. "And the most predictive trait is still demonstrated achievement. But then there are a set of personal characteristics, and the number one most predictive trait is perseverance, or what we would call internal locus of control. People who, in the context of a challenge—and you can't see it unless you're in the context of a challenge—have the instinct to figure out what they can control, and to own it, rather than to blame everyone else in the system. And you can see why in this case. Kids, kids' families, the system—there are so many people to blame. And yet you'll go into the schools and you'll see people teaching in the same hallway, some of whom have that mentality of 'it's not possible to succeed here,' and others who are just prevailing against it all. And it's so much about that mindset—the internal locus of control, and the instinct to stay optimistic in the face of a challenge."

Accenture, the giant consulting firm, has made a science of trying to assess whether candidates have this quality. William D. Green, the CEO of Accenture, said the company considers screening job candidates a core competency, and has developed a system called "critical behavior interviewing" to find the right people. Accenture gets roughly two million résumés a year, and hires between 40,000 and 60,000 people. If it hires well, that gives it a huge competitive advantage. Here's Green explaining Accenture's critical behavior interviewing process:

"It's based on the premise that past behavior is the best indicator of future behavior. Essentially what we're looking for is, have you faced any adversity and what did you do about it? We also know the profile of successful Accenture people, and how do we learn from the people we have who have stayed, learned, grown, and become great leaders, and how do we push that back into the recruiting process to find the best matches for Accenture?

"If you get down to it, it's what have you learned, what have you demonstrated, what behaviors do you have? Have you shown intuition? Have you shown the ability to synthesize and act? Have you shown the ability to step up and make a choice? How have you dealt with the hand in front of you, played it out?"

Green told a story of how one job candidate stood out from the crowd for him.

"I was recruiting at Babson College," he said. "This was in 1991. The last recruit of the day—I get this résumé. I get the blue sheet attached to it, which is the form I'm supposed to fill out with all this stuff. His résumé is very light—no clubs, no sports, no nothing. Babson, 3.2. Studied finance. Work experience: Sam's Diner, references on request. It's the last one of the day, and I've seen all these people come through strutting their stuff and they've got their portfolios and semester studying abroad. Here comes this guy. He sits. His name is Sam, and I say: 'Sam, let me just ask you. What else were you doing while you were here?' He says: 'Well, Sam's Diner. That's our family business, and I leave on Friday after classes, and I go and work till closing. I work all day Saturday till closing, and then I work Sunday until I close, and then I drive back to Babson.' I wrote, 'Hire him,' on the blue sheet. He's still with us, because he had character. He faced a set of challenges. He figured out how to do both. It's work ethic. You could see the guy had charted a path for himself to make it work with the situation he had. He didn't ask for any help. He wasn't victimized by the thing. He just said, 'That's my dad's business, and I work there.' Confident. Proud.

"What critical behavior interviewing does," said Green, "is get at people's character, and you get to see where work fits in their value system, where pride fits in their value system, where making hard decisions or sacrificing fits in their value system. I mean, you sacrifice and you're a victim, or you sacrifice because it's the right thing to do and you have pride in it. Huge difference. Simple thing. Huge difference."

∽

People don't have to climb Mount Everest or run the 135-mile Badwater Ultramarathon through Death Valley to develop battle-hardened confidence. Nor do they need to wish that they had faced more challenges growing up. Battle-hardened confidence starts with the right attitude. And attitude is the one thing that anyone can control, even if it seems like everything else is outside of their control. If you tackle challenges, building a track record of success, then battle-hardened confidence will follow.

A first step, though, requires developing a healthy relationship with failure. Many CEOs recognize that failure is part of success—particularly for people pursuing an ambitious goal—and they embrace failure and value it and learn from it. It can be a hard lesson to learn, particularly for teenagers shifting from high school, where they perhaps grew accustomed to acing exams, to college, and then into their careers.

John Donahoe, the CEO of eBay, said he learned from a mentor how to be more accepting of failure.

"A really valuable piece of advice early in my career was from a guy named Kent Thiry, who was another of my early bosses and is now CEO at DaVita," Donahoe said. "I didn't know it at the time, but I was suffering from a real fear of failure. Kent said, 'You know, John, your challenge is you're trying to bat .900.' And he said, 'When you were in college, you got a lot of A's. You could get 90, 95 percent right. When you took your first job as an analyst, you were really successful and felt like you were batting .900.'

"But he said, and this is probably five years into my career,

'Now you've moved from the minor leagues. You're playing in the major leagues, and if you expect to bat .900, either you come up at bat and freeze because you're so afraid of swinging and missing, or you're a little afraid to step into the batter's box. The best hitters in Major League Baseball, world class, they can strike out six times out of ten and still be the greatest hitters of all time.' That's my philosophy—the key is to get up in that batter's box and take a swing. And all you have to do is hit one single, a couple of doubles, and an occasional home run out of every ten at-bats, and you're going to be the best hitter or the best business leader around. You can't play in the major leagues without having a lot of failures."

Video games have been criticized in some quarters for creating slothful kids. But Jen-Hsun Huang of Nvidia said they taught him a valuable lesson about failure.

"I've never beaten myself up about mistakes," he said. "When I try something and it doesn't turn out, I go back and try it again, and maybe it's because I grew up in the video-game era. Most of the time when you're playing a game you're losing. You lose and lose and lose until you beat it. That's kind of how the game works, right? It's feedback. And then eventually you beat it. As it turns out, the most fun parts of that game are when you're losing. When you finally beat it there's a moment of euphoria, but then it's over. Maybe it's because I grew up in that generation and I have the ability to take chances, which leads to the ability to innovate and try new things. Those are important life lessons that came along."

Learning from failure, and recognizing failure quickly, is part of the culture at Nvidia, Huang said.

"This ability to celebrate failure needs to be an important part of any company that's in a rapidly changing world," he said. "And the second part of our core value is what we characterize as intellectual honesty—the ability to call a spade a spade, to recognize as quickly as possible that we've made a mistake, that we've gone the wrong way, and that we learn from it and quickly adjust. Now it came about because when Nvidia was first founded, we were the first company of our kind, but we rapidly almost went out of business. We built the technology and then it just didn't work. And so we did everything differently.

"It was during that time that I learned that it was okay for a CEO to say that the strategy didn't work, that the technology didn't work, that the product didn't work, but we're still going to be great and let me tell you why. I think that's what's thrilling about leadership. When you're holding on to literally the worst possible hand on the planet and you know you're still going to win. How are you still going to win? Because that's when the character of the company really comes out. And it was during that time that we really cultivated and developed what I consider to be our core values today. I don't think you can create culture and develop core values during great times. I think it's when the company faces adversity of extraordinary proportions, when there's no reason for the company to survive, when you're looking at incredible odds—that's when culture is developed; character is developed.

"And I think 'culture' is a big word for corporate character. It's the personality of the company, and now the personality of our company simply says this: If we think something is really worthwhile to be done and we have a great idea, and it's never been done before but we believe in it, it's okay to take a chance. If it doesn't work, learn from it, adjust, and keep failing forward. But every single time you're making it better and better and better. Before you know it, you're a great company."

John T. Chambers, the CEO of Cisco, said that the adversity

he faced both as a child and as a CEO were among the most important leadership lessons he had learned.

"People think of us as a product of our successes," Chambers said. "I'd actually argue that we're a product of the challenges we faced in life. And how we handled those challenges probably has more to do with what we accomplish in life. I had an issue with dyslexia before they understood what dyslexia was. One of my teachers, Mrs. Anderson, taught me to look at it like a curveball. The ball breaks the same way every time. Once you get used to it, you can handle it pretty well. So I went from almost being embarrassed reading in front of a class—you lose your place, and I read right to left—to the point where I knew I could overcome challenges. I think it also taught me sensitivity toward others.

"I learned another lesson from Jack Welch," he continued. "It was in 1998, and at that time we were one of the most valuable companies in the world. I said, 'Jack, what does it take to have a great company?' And he said, 'It takes major setbacks and overcoming those.' I hesitated for a minute, and I said, 'Well, we did that in '93 and then we did it again in '97 with the Asian financial crisis.' And he said, 'No, John. I mean a near-death experience.' I didn't understand exactly what he meant. Then, in 2001, we had a near-death experience. We went from the most valuable company in the world to a company where they questioned the leadership. And in 2003 he called me up and said, 'John, you now have a great company.' I said, 'Jack, it doesn't feel like it.' But he was right. While it was something I would have given anything to have avoided, it did make us a much better company, a much stronger company, a company that at times doesn't take itself too seriously but also a company that doesn't have fear. We have a lot of healthy paranoia about what can go wrong. So that's a nice way of saying that it's how you lead through tough scenarios that often determines where you go."

Quintin E. Primo III, the co-founder and CEO of Capri Capital, said his experience of surviving a near-death experience also taught him a lot about leadership.

"Leadership, in my opinion, is best learned, or honed, through adversity," he said. "And it's in times of adversity that one must step up to the plate, and do something. You have to do this, or do that, but you just can't stand still. You have to take action in adversity. And for me, probably the most poignant moment in my career as a leader was when my first business failed miserably. We were crushed by the real estate markets of the early '90s. Back then we were a very young, emerging organization with no real business. We entered into a death spiral, roughly two years after I started the firm in '88. And managing down, as the *Titanic* is sinking, you're not even worried about the deck chairs.

"It taught me a lot about who I was. It taught me a great deal about the folks I had selected to work with me on this sinking ship. It was a very frightening period for me, but what I've learned is that one must have faith, faith in something larger than yourself, or you truly will be sunk. Whether that faith is faith in the common good of man, whether it's in universal rhythm or karma, or whether it is simply in God, there has to be something larger than you.

"In that period of adversity for me, I discovered that my employees, as such, were really part of my family. And you will sacrifice, you will do extraordinary things to protect your family, and feed them, and clothe them. You will sacrifice greatly. And so, in this period of adversity, I had to move outside of me. It no longer was all about me, but about making sure that the hardship on those who worked with me was as modest, as low, as possible. It just shifted priorities. After graduating from Harvard Business School, and having success for eight golden years in real estate, I thought I was the next great thing since sliced bread. In abundance, it's very easy to lose focus. But in adversity, one must have extreme focus."

∽

Anyone with a blemish on his résumé or academic record may be tempted to paper over it, or wish it away. That may not be necessary. Many CEOs, and others who have achieved a measure of success in their lives and are in hiring roles, have probably had some rough patches themselves. If candidates can explain what they've learned from those experiences, and how they dealt with them, they may find their résumé goes to the top of the pile.

Meridee A. Moore, the founder of Watershed Asset Management, a hedge fund, said that when she's hiring she considers it a plus when she sees that candidates have suffered a dip in their academic performance at some point, then persevered to improve.

"If you've ever had a setback and come back from it, I think it helps you make better decisions," she said. "There's nothing better for sharpening your ability to predict outcomes than living through some period when things went wrong. You learn that events aren't in your control and no matter how smart you are, and how hard you work, you have to anticipate things that can go against you."

Understand what you can control. Don't be a victim. Figure out a way to get things done. It's a way of perceiving the world that will help you avoid the disappointment of failure, and stay in the right frame of mind for plowing through adversity. Challenges become learning experiences rather than disappointments. It's often just a matter of attitude that makes people stand out. They earn the confidence of their managers that they will take on, and own, any assignment thrown their way.

For bosses, a dream employee will eagerly accept a challenge, and say those words that are music to a manager's ears: "Got it. I'm on it." People who want more responsibility, with a confidence born of a track record of facing down challenges, will move up.

3.

TEAM SMARTS

At some point, the notion of being a team player became devalued in corporate life. Perhaps it was all the rah-rah team-building exercises, the jerseys, the T-shirts, the buttons. They may be good for bonding, but improving teamwork on the job? That takes more work than trust-building exercises like falling backwards into a colleague's arms. The notion of being a team player has been reduced to a truism—I work on a team, therefore I am a team player. It's a point captured in a cartoon, by Mike Baldwin, in which an interviewer says to a job candidate, "We need a dedicated team player. How are you at toiling in obscurity?"

The most effective executives are more than team players. They understand how teams work, the different roles of individual players, and how to get the most out of the group. They know how to create a sense of mission and how to make people feel like everyone's getting credit. They know how to build a sense of commitment in the group. Just as some people have street smarts—they are savvy and know their way around a neighborhood, and they understand the unwritten rules for getting things done—others have team smarts.

In a world in which work is increasingly done through collaboration, team smarts is an essential skill.

"With most of the important things I learned about leadership, it was usually because we weren't hitting our numbers," said Teresa A. Taylor, the chief operating officer of Qwest Communications. "When things are going well, you think, 'Oh good, everything we're doing is right.' When things aren't going so great, that's when you reflect and you say, 'What am I doing that isn't working, or what do I need to change?' It's very much on instinct and experience. Even the instinct is driven by watching people's body language, watching how they're presenting. I mean you can just ask an open-ended question, and if three people wiggle and one person doesn't, you can figure, okay, they're not working together. So I do spend a lot of time reading the room."

It starts with an understanding that teamwork is built on a foundation of one-to-one interactions between people, an unwritten contract that has nothing to do with business cards, organization charts, or titles. A big part of being team smart is appreciating that teamwork is developed by conveying a sense that you are looking out for a colleague, that you've got her back. It's these small exchanges—a favor here, an extra mile of effort there—that become the connective tissue between two people. And that's where teamwork starts: with two people.

Greg Brenneman, the chairman of the private equity firm CCMP Capital, said that one of the most memorable lessons he learned about leadership was from the future Massachusetts governor and presidential candidate Mitt Romney, with whom Brenneman worked at Bain, the consulting firm, long before Romney went into politics.

"He said, 'Greg, in any interaction, you either gain share or lose share. So treat every interaction as kind of a precious moment in time,'" Brenneman recalled. "And I've always remembered that, because I think it's really true. So what I've tried to do is have more conversations where I'm gaining share than losing share, to try to add value to everything."

Gary E. McCullough, the CEO of Career Education Corporation, shared a story that helps bring Brenneman's rule to life. It involved a woman named Rosemary, whom he came to know when he was working at Procter & Gamble. She operated the coffee cart that came around each morning, but McCullough came to appreciate her keen sense of people, and her insights about whether they understood the basics of teamwork.

"Rosemary had an uncanny ability to discern who was going to make it and who wasn't going to make it," McCullough said. "And I remember, when I was probably almost a year into the organization, she told me I was going to be okay. But she also told me some of my classmates who were with the company weren't going to make it. And she was more accurate than the HR organization was. When I talked to her, I said, 'How'd you know?' She could tell just by the way they treated people. In her mind, everybody was going to drop the ball at some point. And then she said, 'You know you're going to drop the ball, and I see that you're good with people and people like you and you treat them right. They're going to pick up the ball for you, and they're going to run and they're going to score a touchdown for you. But if they don't like you, they're going to let that ball lie there and you're going to get in trouble.' Again, I think it's those intangible things."

∾

Being team smart begins with the foundation of learning to work with another person. The next step is to understand team dynamics, and the role that individuals play on each team. Many CEOs have learned these lessons through sports.

Mark Pincus, the CEO of Zynga, the online gaming company, said his experience playing soccer on his school team was a formative leadership lesson.

"We were on the same team together, most of us, for eight or nine years, and we were at a really little school in Chicago that had no chance of really fielding any great athletes," he said. "But we ended up doing really well as a team, and we made it to the state quarterfinals, and it was all because of teamwork. And the one thing I learned from that was that I actually could tell what someone would be like in business, based on how they played on the soccer field. So even today when I play in Sunday-morning soccer games, I can literally spot the people who'd probably be good managers and good people to hire."

He explained the qualities he looked for on the soccer field:

"One is reliability, the sense that they're not going to let the team down, that they're going to hold up their end of the bargain. And in soccer, especially if you play seven on seven, it's more about whether you have seven guys or women who can pull their own weight rather than whether you have any stars. So I'd rather be on a team that has no bad people than a team with stars. There are certain people you just know are not going to make a mistake, even if the other guy's faster than they are, or whatever. They're just reliable.

"And are you a playmaker? There are people who don't want to screw up, and so they just pass the ball right away. Then there are the ones who have this kind of intelligence, and they can make these great plays. These people seem to have high emotional intelligence. It's not that they're star players, but they have decent skills, and they will get you the ball and then be where you'd expect to put it back to them. It's like their heads are really in the game."

Andrew Cosslett of InterContinental Hotels Group also learned about team dynamics from sports—in his case, rugby.

"Everyone's different, so you have to know people," Cosslett said. "I think having a sense of self-awareness is very important, like how you impact each of the people you're with differently. The whole thing about staying alive on a rugby field is about reliance on the guys around you. Each one of those people on a rugby team responds differently because it's physically dangerous as a game. It has a tension in the changing room before you go out to play that's not like any other sport, and I've played lots, because it is almost like going into battle. There's a chance you're going to break your neck or have a very bad injury.

"You need to jell with them as a team, but each one responds individually. So it's about seeing the world on their terms and then dealing with them on their terms, not yours. I think you're born with some of this as well. I'm very sensitive to how people are thinking and feeling at any given moment. That's really helpful in business, because you pick things up very fast."

Part of team building is understanding the roles that different personalities play in a group. For example, Will Wright, the video-game developer behind best-sellers like Spore and The Sims, sees people either as potential "glue" or "solvent" in a team setting when he is considering hiring someone.

"There is the matter of how good is this person, times their teamwork factor," Wright said. "You can have a great person who doesn't really work well on the team, and they're a net loss. You can have somebody who is not that great, but they are really very good glue, so that could be a net gain. A lot of team members I consider glue within the team in that they disseminate things effectively, they motivate and improve the morale of people around them. They basically bring the team tighter and tighter. Others are solvents, and it's their kind of personal nature that they might be disagreeable. They rub people the wrong way. They're always caught in conflicts. For the most part, that is at least as important as their competence in their roles."

Team smarts is about having good peripheral vision for sensing how people react to one another, not just how they act. George S. Barrett, the CEO of Cardinal Health, described an example of how he assessed different managers when he moved into a new role.

"I was running a company that was acquired by a bigger firm," he said. "I stayed with them after the acquisition, and then I got a call from the chairman and he said, 'We're having some issues with our flagship company. Would you be willing to come in and run it?' I was thirty-four years old, and I said to myself, 'Well, it's already struggling. How badly could I mess it up?' So I went there. Everyone on the management team was in their fifties, so the first day I was introduced to them, I thought they were going to collapse. You could sort of see them thinking, 'That kid?'

"I realized I was going to have to win these guys over pretty quickly. I also knew that there were some folks in that group who were probably not going to come along for the ride. It was a turn-around, so I knew that I was going to have to move quickly to fix some things. I was very clear and direct about what I thought we were facing and what we needed to do about it, without blame. I had to create an environment in which people knew it was their job to tell me things that we needed to do because we were going to run out of time. I tend to be very direct. I expect people to be that way with me.

"I concluded fairly quickly that not many of them would be staying. There were some very capable people there, but I just think the employees had lost confidence in them. That's very hard to recover, because so much of leadership is about trust and belief. People have to believe in you. And when they stop believing in you, you can say all the things in the world, but it's very, very hard to mobilize an organization when they've lost that belief."

Barrett said that watching the managers, and watching the organization respond to them, helped him figure out who was going to remain on the team.

"I'll give you an example," he said. "We're sitting with a large group of folks, about forty to fifty managers, and people are standing up to raise certain issues. And I watched this one executive. People were watching and riveted to him, really listening and engaged. And then this other executive spoke, and I watched him address the group, and I watched everyone's eyes. And their eyes went back down to their tables. They couldn't even meet eyes with him. It was a clear signal that said, 'You've lost us.' So sometimes you don't know what the messages are that you're going to get, but you have to look for them. They come from your peripheral vision. And that was one of those cases where I just knew it the second it happened."

How do CEOs build a sense of teamwork, and not just team spirit? Mark Pincus of Zynga used an unusual strategy at one company to encourage each employee to understand his or her individual role better, and to take responsibility for it. He decided to take a more dramatic step after he grew frustrated that too many of his employees were coming to him for answers.

"I'd turn people into CEOs," he said. "One thing I did at my second company was to put white sticky sheets on the wall, and I put everyone's name on one of the sheets, and I said, 'By the end of the week, everybody needs to write what you're CEO of, and it needs to be something really meaningful.' And that way, everyone knows who's CEO of what and they know whom to ask instead of me. And it was really effective. People liked it. And there was nowhere to hide.

"We had this really motivated, smart receptionist. She was young. We kept outgrowing our phone systems, and she kept coming back and saying, 'Mark, we've got to buy a whole new phone system.' And I said, 'I don't want to hear about it. Just buy it. Go figure it out.' She spent a week or two meeting every vendor and figuring it out. She was so motivated by that. I think that was a big lesson for me because what I realized was that if you give people really big jobs to the point that they're scared, they have way more fun and they improve their game much faster. She ended up running our whole office."

Nell Minow of The Corporate Library said her best lesson for building a sense of teamwork is to organize a group around a simple word: *we.*

"The first time I ever really thought of myself as a leader was when I had a series of experiences in college, over a period of about eighteen months, working on four different group projects," Minow said. "What I learned from that is if you can get everyone to agree what the goal is, and to identify themselves with the successful achievement of that goal, then you're pretty much there. One thing that helped move my thinking forward was that I noticed in my first job that there was something very definitional in who was included in somebody's 'we' and who was included in somebody's 'them.' I found generally that the more expansive the assumptions were within somebody's idea of who 'we' is—the larger the group you include in that 'we'—the better off everybody was. I started to really do my best to make sure that my notion of 'we' was very expansive and to promote that idea among other people."

Another key strategy for building a sense of teamwork is learning to share credit.

"I was a mechanic in the Navy," said Gordon Bethune, the former CEO of Continental Airlines. "And mechanics in the Navy are like mechanics in airlines. You may have more stripes than I do, but you don't know how to fix the airplane. You want me to fix it? You know how much faster I could fix the airplane when I wanted to, than when I didn't want to? So I've always felt that if you treat me with respect, I'll do more for you. As I went up the ladder in the Navy, I never forgot what it's like to be down the ladder, and that being good at your job is predicated pretty much on how the people working for you feel. Here's my theory: Let's say we're all mid-level managers, and one VP slot is going to open up. I've got ten guys working for me, and for the last five years, every time I got any recognition, I said, 'Bring them on the stage with me.' Who do you think is going to get the job? I'm going to get the job."

Teamwork can be built by being explicit about the roles people play, and insisting on rules and routines. Jilly Stephens, the executive director of City Harvest, a nonprofit organization that helps feed the hungry in New York, learned this lesson when she had a leadership position in her twenties at Orbis International, where she had responsibility for coordinating the medical teams aboard a "hospital with wings"—a plane that flew around to developing countries to perform eye surgeries.

"It was a lot of responsibility, and I guess it was a sort of sink-or-swim moment," she said. "I had to lead that group, and it was complicated by the fact that it was multinational, so at its peak I think I was dealing with eleven or twelve nationalities. We were probably about thirty to thirty-five people. It was constantly focusing on teamwork. The way we did it was just being really rigorous about routine and, in some ways, not that flexible, so people really knew what the ground rules were. One example—and it seems so matronly now that I look back on it—was that the team had to be in the lobby at the hotel, ready to go to work, at whatever the designated time was. If they weren't there, the bus leaves. You get to the airport yourself. If we were in Tunisia, that meant finding a bike and cycling across the desert to get to the airport. When I first got to the field, you would have the nurses, engineers, whoever, waiting, and you would maybe have one who just couldn't drag himself out of bed and everybody's waiting. We saw behaviors change fairly rapidly. So we had a fairly tight routine, and we made announcements every morning. It was just important to let everybody know what was coming."

Sharon Napier, the CEO of the advertising agency Partners + Napier, played basketball in high school and college, and she uses sports analogies constantly with her staff to drive home messages, including the notion that people have roles to play, that the team's success is what matters most.

"I went from playing high school basketball to college basketball," she said. "You can be a star in high school, and you can be the ninth player in college. It's just the way it is. So I always talk about understanding the bench strength. First of all, every player has a role. Know what it is. If you're the seventh player who's supposed to go in and get five rebounds because we need them, that's your role. So I talk about that a lot—we don't have the starting team and the not-starting team. We have a bench, and everybody has to be strong. They come in and they bring different things to the table. And you learn that by playing. You learn that if you're not worried about your own success, and you're worried about the success of the team, you go a lot further."

Perhaps one of the simplest ways to think about teamwork is to forget organizational charts and titles. Companies increasingly operate through ad hoc teams, formed and disbanded to accomplish various tasks. Team smarts refers to this ability to recognize the type of players the team needs, and how to bring them together around a common goal. Susan Lyne, the CEO of Gilt Groupe, said the ultimate test of team smarts today is being able to bring together a group of people, including those who don't report directly to you. Lyne described how she grew to appreciate team players, and what they can and should bring to the table.

"I think that now I have a very strong antenna for someone who is going to be poison within a company," she said. "I think that early on, I was wowed by talent, and I was willing to set aside the idea that this person might not be a team player. Now, somebody needs to be able to work with people—that's number one on the list. I need people who are going to be able to build a team, manage a team, recruit well, and work well with their peers. And that's another thing you learn over time. Somebody may be a great manager of a team, but incapable of working across the company to get things done because they're competitive, or because of any number of reasons. Can they manage down? Can they work across the company and get people to want to work with them and to help them succeed? And are they going to keep you well informed of everything that's going on?"

Lyne said this skill is so crucial today that business schools should be teaching it in more courses.

"There are a lot of great courses on managing or developing a strategic agenda, but there is very little about how to work with your peers where you need to get X done, and you need these other three departments to give you X amount of time in order to succeed at that. The people who truly succeed in business are the ones who actually have figured out how to mobilize people who are not their direct reports. Everyone can get their direct reports to work for them, but getting people who do not have to give you their time to engage and to support you and to want you to succeed is something that is sorely missing from B-school courses."

4.

A SIMPLE MINDSET

Here's a hypothetical test that can speed the process of identifying who has what it takes to move up in an organization.

Imagine giving one hundred vice presidents the same task: take a month to search out a new business opportunity for their company, and then present the idea to a group of senior executives during a weekend off-site meeting. The month passes, they have their ideas, and the day arrives to start their presentations.

The ideas are all pretty good, but the presentations vary enormously in length. One by one, the young vice presidents come in. Some want to take forty-five minutes, using a thirty-slide Power-Point deck to pitch their idea. Other presentations are shorter, with only ten slides. Still others have three slides or even two, and they're done in five minutes or less. One person doesn't use Power-Point at all. She simply talks, giving a short pitch for her idea, backed up with three key facts.

The executives are impressed by how concise she was, the simplicity of the idea, and that she respected their time. Later, she gets a call. The executives want to sign her up for the company's leadership development program for high-potential employees.

$\sim$

There is a stubborn disconnect in many companies. By all accounts, CEOs—and most senior executives—want the same thing from people who present to them: be concise, be brief, get to the point, make it simple. Business is not always as complicated as it sometimes appears to be, nor should it be.

"I've tried to do less of the things that make business more complex," said Eduardo Castro-Wright, a vice chairman at Wal-Mart Stores. "I really like simplicity. At the end of the day, retailing—though you could apply this to many other businesses—is not as complicated as we would like to make it. It is pretty logical and simple, if you think about the way that you yourself would act, or do act, as a customer."

Yet few people can deliver the simplicity that many bosses want. Instead, they mistakenly assume the bosses will be impressed by a long PowerPoint presentation that shows how diligently they researched a topic, or that they will win over their superiors by talking more, not less.

Few things seem to get CEOs riled up more than lengthy PowerPoint presentations. It's not the software they dislike—it's just a tool, after all. What irks them is the unfocused thinking that leads to an overlong slide presentation. There is wide agreement it's a problem—"Death by PowerPoint" has become a cliché.

If so many executives in positions of authority are clear about what they want, why can't they get the people who report to them to lose the "Power" part of their presentations and simply get to the "Point"?

There are a few likely explanations. The first is that a lot of people have trouble being concise. Next time you're in a meeting, ask somebody to give you the ten-word summary of his or her idea. Some people can do a quick bit of mental jujitsu, and they'll summarize an idea with a "Here's what's important . . ." or "The bottom line is . . ." Even if they take twenty-five words, they at least understand what's being asked of them.

Others will pause for a moment and then launch into a lengthy discussion of the idea, because they have trouble identifying the core point. Granted, it's not easy—a point that's been captured in many sayings through the ages. "Simplicity is the ultimate sophistication," said Leonardo da Vinci. And in words attributed to Mark Twain (and many others), "I didn't have time to write a short letter, so I wrote a long one instead."

Another possible explanation is that a lag exists in the business world. There was a time when simply having certain information was a competitive advantage. Now, in the Internet era, with oceans of data available to all with just a few clicks of a mouse and keyboard, others can get easy access to the same information. That puts a greater premium on the ability to synthesize, to connect dots in new ways, and to ask the simple, smart question that leads to an untapped opportunity.

"I'd love to teach a course called 'The Idea,'" said Dany Levy, the founder of DailyCandy.com. "Which is basically, so you want to start a company, how's it going to work? Let's figure it out—just a very practical plan, but not a business plan, because I feel like business plans now feel weighty and outdated. It seems, back in the day, that the longer your business plan was, the more promising it was going to be. And now, the shorter your business plan is, the more succinct and to the point it is, the better. You want people to get why your business is going to work pretty quickly."

"Schools could do a better job teaching the value of brevity," said Guy Kawasaki, the co-founder of Alltop, a news aggregation site, and managing director of Garage Technology Ventures.

"What you learn in school is the opposite of what happens in the real world," he said. "In school, you're always worried about minimums. You have to reach twenty pages or have so many slides or whatever. Then you get out in the real world and you think, 'I have to have a minimum of twenty pages and fifty slides.' They should teach students how to communicate in five-sentence e-mails and with ten-slide PowerPoint presentations. If they just taught every student that, American business would be much better off. No one wants to read *War and Peace* e-mails. Who has the time? Ditto with sixty PowerPoint slides for a one-hour meeting."

Steven A. Ballmer, the CEO of Microsoft, said he understands the impulse to share all the underlying research that led to a conclusion. But he changed the way he runs meetings to get to the conclusion first.

"The mode of Microsoft meetings used to be: You come with something we haven't seen in a slide deck or presentation. You deliver the presentation. You probably take what I will call 'the long and winding road.' You take the listener through your path of discovery and exploration, and you arrive at a conclusion. That's kind of the way I used to like to do it, and the way Bill Gates used to kind of like to do it. And it seemed like the best way to do it, because if you went to the conclusion first, you'd get: 'What about this? Have you thought about this?' So people naturally tried to tell you all the things that supported the decision, and then tell you the decision.

"I decided that's not what I want to do anymore. I don't think it's productive. I don't think it's efficient. I get impatient. So most meetings nowadays, you send me the materials and I read them in advance. And I can come in and say: 'I've got the following four questions. Please don't present the deck.' That lets us go, whether they've organized it that way or not, to the recommendation. And if I have questions about the long and winding road and the data and the supporting evidence, I can ask them. But it gives us greater focus."

∾

Some CEOs put strict limits on PowerPoint slides. The rule, of course, is a way to force people to put in the time and energy to sort out what's truly important and what's extraneous. Sometimes this work is most effectively done away from a computer. A blank piece of paper. A pencil. These are the only tools that really matter for what is often the most difficult step: thinking.

"I say, 'Three slides, three points,'" said James Schiro of Zurich Financial Services. "You really can't manage more than three or four things at the most, but I like to see it in three slides. I hate Power-Point presentations. If you're working in an area, and you are running a business, you ought to be able to stand up there and tell me about your business without referring to a big slide deck. When you are speaking, people should focus on you and focus on the message. They can't walk away remembering a whole bunch of different things, so you have to have three or four really key messages that you take them through, and you remind them of what's important."

Simplifying the complex is the CEO's job, and CEOs do it all day long. They are paid to create order out of chaos, to identify the three or five things employees need to focus on rather than twenty things that will send people off in different directions. They want to avoid the corporate equivalent of that expression frequently heard on the golf course—paralysis by analysis.

"Even before I go into a company," said Greg Brenneman of CCMP Capital, "or even if we're looking at a business here at CCMP, I'm constantly asking the question, 'What are the two or three levers that, if done right, if pulled correctly, will really turn this business?' Then I take that and put it into a one-page plan. If I can't simply put what needs to be done on one page, I probably haven't thought it through very well. I learned back in the days when I was consulting at Bain & Company—and before that when I was at Harvard Business School doing case studies—that they give you more information than you could possibly read. So you needed to quickly step back and say, 'What are the two or three things that really matter?' And I find in the world that people don't really do that often. They just dive into all this detail and start using acronyms and buzzwords and they don't step back. When one of our guys is presenting an investment, you always kind of know they have it if they can explain it very quickly. And if it takes a really long time and you're into the square root of the price of oil in Uzbekistan, you probably know that it's gotten too complicated, and that's when I start asking questions—when people start having trouble simply saying, 'Here's the idea.'"

William Green of Accenture offers a telling example of the art of simplification. He shared the story of how he once sat through a three-day training session for new managers. He said he counted sixty-eight things that the managers were told they needed to do to be successful—"everything from how you coach and mentor to your annual reviews, filling out these forms, all this stuff.

"And I got up to close the session, and I'm thinking about how it isn't possible for these people to remember all this. So I said there are three things that matter. The first is competence—just being good at what you do, whatever it is, and focusing on the job you have, not on the job you think you want to have. The second one is confidence. People want to know what you think. So you have to have enough desirable self-confidence to articulate a point of view. The third thing is caring. Nothing today is about one individual. This is all about the team, and in the end, this is about giving a damn about your customers, your company, the people around you, and recognizing that the people around you are the ones who make you look good. When young people are looking for clarity—this is a huge, complex global company, and they wonder how to navigate their way through it—I just tell them that."

Tachi Yamada, the president of the Bill and Melinda Gates Foundation's Global Health Program, said that this ability to spot the key levers in any project or plan is vital for executives as they get further away from doing the work itself, and more into a management role where they must delegate. Yamada advocates for an alternative approach to micromanagement: what he calls "micro-interest." A prerequisite for that is being able to quickly figure out the two or three things that matter in any project.

"I think the most difficult transition for anybody from being a worker bee to a manager is this issue of delegation," he said. "What do you give up? How can you have the team do what you would do yourself without your doing it? If you're a true micromanager and you basically stand over everybody and guide their hands to do everything, you don't have enough hours in the day to do what the whole team needs to do.

"Learning how to delegate, learning how to let go and still make sure that everything happened, was a very important lesson in my first role in management. And that's where I learned a principle that I apply today—I don't micromanage, but I have micro-interest. I do know the details. I do care about the details. I feel like I have intimate knowledge of what's going on, but I don't tell people what to do. Every day I read about a thousand pages of documents, whether grants or letters or scientific articles, or whatever. I have learned what the critical things to read are. If there are ten tasks in an overall project, what is the most critical task among those ten? What is the one thing that everything else hinges on? And what I'll do is I'll spend a lot of time understanding that one thing. Then, when the problem occurs, it usually occurs there, and I can be on top of what the problem is. It's just having enough experience to understand when problems do occur and how they occur, why they occur, and being prepared for that particular problem. Problems can occur in the other ten areas, but they won't determine the outcome of the overall project. But there may be one or two points where the outcome of the entire project is at stake, and you'd better be on top of it."

Meridee Moore of Watershed Asset Management looks for that ability to simplify when she's assessing job candidates.

"We give people a two-hour test," she said. "We try to simulate a real office experience by giving them an investment idea and the raw material, the annual report, some documents, and then we tell them where the securities prices are. We say, 'Here's a calculator, a pencil, and a sandwich. We'll be back in two hours.' If an analyst comes in there and just attacks the project with relish, that's a good sign. After two hours, two of us go in and just let the person talk about what he's done. The nice thing about my being trained as a lawyer, and never going to business school, is that I'm able to ask the basic financially naïve questions, like: 'What does the company do? How do they make money? Who are their customers? What do they make? How do they produce it?' That throws some people off.

"Often, analysts go right to the financials and forget to think about the company's business model. If the person avoids answering the basic questions and instead changes the subject to talk about the work they did, that tells me the person is a bit rigid. Instead of trying to respond to what's being asked, they're trying to get an A on the test. Also, if they're a little too worried about pleasing me, that's not good, either, because it's not a please-the-boss competition. The point of the exercise is to make sure that we've thought about the issues critically, so we are in a position to make a good investment decision. The other quality we look for is whether the person can distill a lot of very complicated information down to its essence. Can you figure out the three or four issues that are most important for understanding this investment? Or do you get distracted by aspects of the company that really have nothing to do with making an investment or determining value?"

Identifying the three or five facts that matter is a first step. Connecting them in a way that tells a story makes for even more effective presentations, CEOs said.

"I believe, and this is the storyteller in me and maybe the former newspaper reporter, that I'd much rather have someone write a two-page summary of what they're thinking," said James E. Rogers, the CEO of Duke Energy. "When you're forced to sit and write it, not only are you getting the subject, verb, predicates right, but you're tying the sentences together and ideas together. When you actually have to write something, you start to develop a more cohesive logic.

"I think words really make a difference—what you say, how you say it. A lot of energy needs to go into how you present the idea. And I'm not talking about spin, I'm really talking about making the idea come alive through a story. It's the ability to pull the salient facts together and tell a story, so that people feel it, sense it, they're convinced by it, and want to do something because of it. In a sense, as a CEO, part of my job is not only to help develop direction but to teach storytelling."

People who are concise and clear in their presentations are heroes to time-pressed colleagues and bosses.

"I use a little saying, which is, 'Be brief, be bright and be gone,'" said Teresa Taylor of Qwest Communications. "It's also not uncommon for me to say, 'Why don't we put the PowerPoint aside for a minute and why don't you just talk to me?' I'd rather just talk. A really great meeting, to me, is someone who is just talking to me and might give me a piece of paper or two to support something, but that's it. I think the world of the person. I just want to thank them."

And, most likely, promote that person.

5.

FEARLESSNESS

Are you comfortable being uncomfortable? Do you get bored when things seem too settled? Do you like situations where there's no road map or compass? Do you start twitching when things are operating smoothly, and want to shake things up? Are you willing to make surprising career moves to learn new skills? Is discomfort your comfort zone?

In other words, are you fearless?

Risk-taking is often a quality associated with entrepreneurs, the kind of people who have the stomach to make bet-the-farm wagers on a new business idea and are held up as heroes in business magazines for their bold moves. But risk-taking doesn't quite capture the quality that many CEOs embody and look for and encourage in others. With the business world in seemingly endless turmoil, maintaining the status quo—even when things appear to be working well—is only going to put you behind the competition. So when

CEOs talk about executives on their staffs who are fearless, there is a reverence in their voices. They wish they could bottle it and pass it out to all their employees, a kind of Gatorade to get everybody moving and taking action. They're looking for calculated and informed risk-taking, but mostly they want people to do things—and not just what they're told to do. It's only natural that many people gravitate to their comfort zones, and in response many CEOs try to create a culture of action, in which employees are encouraged to make decisions that are outside the strategy playbook.

"One of the things that I characterize as fearlessness," said Ursula Burns of Xerox, "is seeing an opportunity, even though things are not broken. The company is not headed toward a wall. It's not broken, but there is definitely a way to do it better and someone will actually say, 'Things are good, but I'm going to destabilize them because they can be much better and should be much better.' One of the guys I characterize as very fearless is somebody we've given a huge amount of responsibility to, running manufacturing and supply chain operations. He continuously pushes. He says, 'So it's running fairly well. We're getting all the machines into place, but we should change this. We should do this.' And he's fearless in destabilizing things to make them better and making decisions and making choices. That's what I mean by fearlessness. Because the easiest thing to do is to just keep it going the way it's going, especially if it's not perfect but it's not broken. But you have to be a little bit ahead of it, and you have to try to fix it well before you have to. Companies get into trouble when they get really complacent, when they settle in and say, 'Okay, we're doing okay now.'

"When you have good, you can actually talk yourself out of great," Burns said, invoking the book *Good to Great* by Jim Collins. "But if you're fearless, you can take on a bit of a risk to change things for the better."

Fearlessness can be learned. Many CEOs found they had to adjust to a fact of life about the chief executive job—that the CEO often has to make a decision sooner than she would otherwise like to because she would prefer to have more time or information. Debra L. Lee, the CEO of BET Networks, had to adjust her comfort zone when she moved from being the firm's general counsel to chief operating officer.

"As general counsel, you're taught research, research, find out every case, find out every opinion, think about it," she said. "It's almost like you're a judge. So when I went from being general counsel to COO, that's the way I first approached it. I'd go into senior staff meetings and I'd listen to advertising and sales folks, I'd listen to the programmers, I'd listen to everyone. And then my job was to go away, think about it and make a decision. Well, that doesn't work. By that time, they're all going off in five different directions. I had to learn to make decisions quicker, on the spot, and follow my gut. You're not going to have all the information. You're not going to be able to run the numbers and come up with the perfect answers."

Gary McCullough of Career Education Corporation said the pressure to make decisions, even when there is a dearth of data for making them, was among the biggest surprises he encountered when he first moved into the corner office.

"One is the breadth of topics or issues that you're confronted with on a daily basis," he said. "You have to be able to go from one thing to another to another, and sometimes it feels like they're completely unrelated. In some cases, it's a snap decision. It's got to be 'This is how we're going to proceed, move forward' versus taking time to really contemplate the question. So if you're not comfortable with dealing in gray areas or you're not comfortable with deciding with 75 or 80 percent of the data you would want to have, then this is not a job that people should aspire to."

∽

Many executives said that fearlessness—a willingness to shake up their lives and their jobs—is one of the top qualities they're looking for when they are interviewing job candidates.

"You have to have people in an organization who are willing to truly embrace change," said Tachi Yamada of the Bill and Melinda Gates Foundation's Global Health Program. "Because if they don't, then what you have is an organization that's constantly fighting to stay at the status quo. And that leads to stagnation. It's also an unsustainable model. I've made an observation about people. There are people who have moved. Take somebody who's a child of an Army officer—they will have moved ten times in their lives. And then there are people who've been born and raised and educated and employed in one town their whole lives. Who do you think is willing to change? I think, in this modern world, you really have to be sure that your workforce has the experience of being elsewhere. That experience gives you the ability to be comfortable with change. The biggest problems I see in a group of people who don't embrace change is that they will always fight anything new, any new idea, any new concept, any outside point of view. And there are many examples of companies that have failed because of that. So I think that's a critical point. Almost all of the people on our staff have traveled all around the world, have lived everywhere."

Mindy Grossman, the CEO of HSN, the parent company of Home Shopping Network, likes to see evidence of risk-taking in the resumes of job candidates.

"They've had to put themselves in a situation, whether they

took a lateral move to get to the next step or they went to a company that wasn't performing, and it was their first opportunity to manage a team that had to do a turnaround," she said. "Specifically, in this culture I have to have people who not only can manage change but have an appetite for it. I love asking people how they made their career decisions, why they made those decisions. What I find is that a lot of people I relate to or even work with have taken segues like that. They tend to be more intellectually curious, so they don't just have vertical climbs. I ask for those stories. I love hearing them and it gives me a real sense of the person."

Anne Mulcahy, former CEO of Xerox, talked about this quality in the context of her own career path, and also how she hired new executives. The qualities she wanted to see were adaptability and flexibility.

"One of the things that is mind-boggling right now is how much we have to change all the time," she said. "For anybody who's into comfort and structure, it gets harder and harder to feel satisfied in the company. It's almost like you have to embrace a lot of ambiguity and be adaptable and not get into the rigidness or expectation-setting that I think there used to be ten years ago, when you could kind of plot it out and define where you were going to go. I think it's a lot more fluid right now. It has to be. The people who really do the best are those who actually sense it, almost enjoy that lack of definition around their roles and what they can contribute."

She searched for that quality partly by studying a candidate's work experience.

"I'm looking for how much breadth someone's had, and their appetite for not just vertical career ladders but their appetite for what I call the horizontal experiences, where it wasn't always just about a title or the next layer up," she said. "And there was this desire to learn new things, to kind of grab on to things that were maybe even somewhat nontraditional. Those kinds of experiences I think bode well for someone who's going to be open and adaptive in this job environment."

Mulcahy's own career trajectory reflects a degree of fearlessness.

"I had come up through the sales organization and I was very much a product of that—you know, the next level of upward mobility," she said. "I reached a point where I felt like I was running out of steam, and I knew that you can always get bigger and bigger budgets and sales assignments. But I chose to go into human resources. I didn't do it so much because of leadership development or career aspirations. I did it simply because I thought it was really interesting. I'd always believed that human resources could be a very powerful part of an organization and often wasn't. So I kind of threw my hat in that ring, wound up running human resources for Xerox worldwide. That was a decision that certainly changed my career path and reinforced the power of leadership for me."

Like the other four keys to success, fearlessness is an attitude, and because attitude is one of the few things over which everyone has complete control, it is a character trait that can be developed. It can be fostered with a simple approach to taking more risks. It is a habit of mind many CEOs share.

"I try to get out of my comfort zone every day," said Steve Hannah, CEO of The Onion. "I say yes to things that I really don't want to do, or I get involved in things that are difficult for me to be involved in, for whatever reason."

CEOs advise that you will be rewarded for fearlessness, because so few people live that way and bring this attitude to work. It is risky. You may unsettle people by shaking up the status quo. But if you have the best interests of the organization in mind, you can unlock new opportunities for the company. And for yourself.

❧

Remember that group of one hundred executives, all around age thirty-five, whom we met at the beginning of chapter 1? Fast-forward twenty years later. They are all in their mid-fifties. Several of them have moved up to the highest ranks of the organization, thanks to a strong track record of proving to their bosses, day in and day out, that they have what it takes to help the company succeed. They are passionately curious about the entire organization and how it can beat the competition. They have shown repeatedly that they can tackle tough assignments. They have built teams of complementary staff and rallied them around ambitious goals. They have distilled complex strategy decisions down to just a few priorities, helping align their employees around just a handful of focused goals. And they have pushed and prodded their bosses to shake up the organization, taking bold steps even when there was no burning need to do so. These are the people you find at the top of organizations. They embody these qualities and, as leaders, help develop them in others.

6.

PREPARATION, PATIENCE, AND OBSTACLE COURSES

Career management. Career ladder.

These phrases have been used for decades to frame discussions about work. They persist, for obvious reasons. "Career management," after all, implies that you can "manage" your career in the same way you can manage your household budget. Plan carefully, the phrase suggests, and you will get what you want. And the "career ladder"? That's an enticing idea, too. Just step on the first rung, work hard, and begin a smooth and steady climb to the top job. The path is clear, and the destination is obvious.

There's just one problem with these notions. The world doesn't actually work this way.

A different metaphor better reflects how people should think about their professional lives—as an obstacle course, filled with surprises, ups and downs, and lateral moves. And plenty of other people are on the course, too.

Barbara J. Krumsiek, the CEO of the Calvert Group, an investment firm, started using the obstacle-course analogy after she decided that the old notions didn't work.

"I believe that the whole career ladder concept is a very disruptive concept, because what does it suggest?" she said. "You can't get past the person ahead of you unless you push them off the ladder. It promotes aggressive behavior. When you think of an obstacle course, there are a lot of people on the obstacle course at the same time, and my success doesn't impede your success. And I may be able to take a minute and help you over that next obstacle and still get where I want to get to."

Krumsiek, like other CEOs, has a great vantage point from which to offer career advice. These top executives know what got them to the corner office, and they can see what has worked for others in their organizations, since they often play a direct role—certainly at senior levels—in deciding who gets promoted.

Much of the CEOs' advice for succeeding on the career obstacle course falls into two broad categories: preparation and patience.

Prepare for a career, they say, don't plan it. By focusing on gaining broad experience, you will be better prepared for any opportunities that arise. Be patient, too—focus on doing your current job well and promotions will come; unbridled ambition is more likely to turn bosses off rather than impress them. And be open to the serendipity that arises from building relationships— chance meetings can lead to new opportunities you never expected, and if you have blinders on as you relentlessly pursue your career plan, you may miss those opportunities. Push yourself out of your comfort zone, perhaps even leaving the country, so that you learn more about other cultures as well as about yourself.

Preparation

Carol Bartz of Yahoo prefers the metaphor of a pyramid rather than a "career ladder," because it sends a signal that people should build a broad and solid base of experience from which to move up.

"I wasn't given this advice, but this is what happened in my life," she said. "You need to build your career not as a ladder, but as a pyramid. You need to have a base of experience because it's a much more stable structure. Think about it. If you've done a lot of different jobs, you've got a platform to go up, however high it is you want to go. What that involves is taking lateral moves, and it involves getting out of your comfort zone. Everybody wants to always progress, always progress. Am I moving upward and onward? But who's going to move upward and onward for forty straight years in a career? And yet the business schools kind of portray it that way. That's not how it works. Go find out how companies run."

David Novak of Yum Brands echoed Bartz's suggestion about the need to learn how an entire organization works, not just mastering a particular specialty. That interest will also create new opportunities to get to know people throughout the organization— relationships that can prove valuable later on.

"I tell people that once you get a job you should act like you run the place," he said. "Not in terms of ego, but in terms of how you think about the business. Don't just think about your piece of the business. Think about your piece of the business and the total business. This way, you'll always represent a broader perspective."

It's not easy to let go of time-honored notions about careers. It's natural for people to think that if they don't land the right first job at the perfect company out of college, then they will either fall behind or take themselves out of the running for important opportunities in life. Yet nearly all CEOs say that such worries are ultimately a waste of time and create unnecessary stress.

Omar Hamoui, who dropped out of the Wharton business school to start AdMob, the mobile advertising network, said he saw far too much fretting among new graduates.

"Don't be afraid," Hamoui said. "What I mean by that is lots and lots of decisions are made by fear and they're made by people who think they have more to lose than they actually have to lose. When you're just graduating from college, there are so many people who want to start something. I mean, ultimately, if it doesn't work out, if they were employable in the first place, they'll still be employable afterward, and they'll be able to do something. They aren't going to live in a cardboard box in the street.

"I think business school students are comical in this area. If you go to business school or law school or any professional school with these highly motivated people, they are stressed out of their minds. Like, they're going to be homeless if they don't get an internship in the summer. You're going to be okay. But everybody has a very hard time calculating the actual risk. They are too afraid of things. Or even when they're at a job, they might have a controversial point of view or make a controversial decision, and they're so scared of getting fired that they don't actually try and act on that. I think that's harder to say in this environment, given the economy and where unemployment is. Perhaps that uncertainty needs to factor into people's risk assessment. But on the whole, many professional people are more worried and more afraid than they should be."

Barbara Krumsiek of the Calvert Group echoed the advice of many CEOs for new graduates: Don't worry so much about your first job out of college.

"You are not going to know where you're going to wind up," she said. "So if you think it's all about researching and finding the exact right place for you, forget about it. I thought I was going to go on and get a PhD in math and teach. You never know. So I try to help young people think about not putting too much weight on it. Just try to get a job that looks interesting. You want to be part of a good company. That's important. But if you can get a foot in the door at a good company and a job that's moderately interesting, it doesn't have to be the last job of your life. And you can learn an awful lot about who you are. There's no way that an undergraduate education teaches you anything about the working world."

Guy Kawasaki of Alltop and Garage Technology Ventures also encourages people not to worry so much about the jobs they have in their twenties.

"Most people who graduate from college think they have to make a perfect choice," he said. "Is it Goldman Sachs? Is it Google? Is it Apple? They think that their first job is going to determine their career, if not their life. Looking back, that's absolutely incorrect."

Kawasaki said that the most important thing is to focus on learning experiences.

"Let's say you land in a start-up, and it becomes the next Google," he said. "Now you're twenty-five years old, and you're worth fifty million dollars. Anybody would call that a success. But let's say you join a start-up, and it implodes. You would learn more about leadership inside a company that crashes than you would inside the next Google. Specifically, you will learn what not to do. You can't make a mistake as a college graduate."

Kawasaki spoke from experience—his first job was far from the world of technology.

"I started my career counting diamonds and schlepping gold jewelry around the world," he said. "The jewelry business is a very,

very tough business—tougher than the computer business. You truly have to understand how to take care of your customers. I learned a very valuable lesson: how to sell. Sales is everything. As long as you're making sales, you're still in the game. That lesson has stuck with me throughout my career."

Several CEOs mentioned selling as an important skill that can pay off throughout a career.

"My advice to young people is always, along the way, have a sales job," said Cristóbal Conde, the CEO of SunGard, the software and IT services firm. "You could be selling sweaters. You could be selling ice cream on the street. It doesn't matter. Selling something to somebody who doesn't want to buy it is a lifelong skill. I can tell when somebody comes in for an interview and they've never had any responsibility for sales."

Whether it's sales or other skills, the point is to view jobs as learning experiences that will broaden knowledge and open up new opportunities and relationships. In today's turbulent global economy, a broad base of experience can be the best job security.

"As you think about your career, it's not about planning it," said Clarence Otis Jr., the CEO of Darden Restaurants, recalling important advice he was given. "Things are too dynamic; there's too much going on; there are too many things that'll pop up, good and bad. It's not about planning and career planning; it's about preparation and building skills. And if you do that, then you'll recover from the mishaps, and you'll be able to take advantage of the opportunities."

Several CEOs said that travel is the best preparation for a career.

"Three words: leave the country," said Quintin Primo of Capri Capital. "Get out of here. That's what I tell everybody—just go. I don't care where you go, just go. Because the world is changing. It is no longer acceptable to speak only English if you are twenty-five and younger. It's unacceptable. You have little chance of being successful if you speak only one language.

"So you've got to get out of your front door, get out of the comfort and quiet of your home and your safety zone, and step into a pool of risk where you have no idea what the outcome is going to be. Out of it all, you will have a much broader understanding of the world's cultures, and you will have a much clearer idea of how the world perceives our culture, and all the value and the benefits and the beauty of our culture. There is nothing more important. I don't care where you went to business school. I don't care whether your grades were good or bad. You have to leave the country."

Andrew Cosslett of InterContinental Hotels Group offers similar advice.

"Leave home," he said. "Go as far away as possible from what you know. I think you've got to be tested, and you've got to test yourself. So my best career advice would be life advice. Go and find out who you are and what you can deal with and put yourself in some positions that will be distinctly uncomfortable. Forcing yourself out of your comfort zone is a great lesson in life."

Patience

In business, patience can get a bad reputation. If a company lets a competitor get a half-step jump on a new market shift, it can find itself playing catch-up. Better to be bold, to take risks, to get to new markets first. Many entrepreneurs are lauded for their impatience—it's their hard-charging attitude that helped them win the race. "If you're not the lead dog, the view never changes," as the saying goes.

So it can be hard to counsel ambitious people to be patient in their careers. Yet that is precisely the advice that many CEOs offer.

"When it comes to managing a career, patience is extremely important because people set goals for themselves that often are unrealistic," said Robert Iger of Disney. "It's great to do that because you want to be ambitious, but you don't have control of a lot of circumstances. And when you set these goals and they're not met, the reasons are beyond your control, it creates impatience and you then make career decisions out of impatience. That's a big mistake. One of my bosses once said that just when you think nothing's going to change, everything changes. And you reach a point where you're not sure any opportunity is going to present itself, and the next day you come in, and *boom*—you're smacked in the face with some huge new opportunity you didn't even predict was going to occur. That happened to me a number of times."

CEOs also say they appreciate people who focus on doing the job they have now, and frown on people who seem more concerned about the day when they can order business cards with some new title. Do the work well, they say, and the promotions will follow.

Andrew Cosslett of InterContinental Hotels Group said that letting go of specific career expectations can make people more effective in their current roles because they're more willing to shake up the status quo.

"Keep asking questions," said Cosslett. "There's a lot of perceived wisdom in most industries that hasn't been challenged for years. The trick in business is not to care too much. Because if you care too much, you won't ask questions and you won't challenge because you'll care too much about your position and what someone's thinking about you. I was always relatively cavalier in my early career because I always thought if I don't make it in business, I'll go and do something else anyway. I always have given 100 percent to everything I've done, but I've always had a slightly maverick side that actually stood me in great stead because it enabled me to ask those difficult questions and be the burr under the saddle."

Gary McCullough of Career Education Corporation said many business school graduates enter the workforce with unrealistic expectations about how quickly they will rise in an organization.

"It does take a little while to get a job like mine," he said. "I can't tell you the number of young people who think that they're going to end up with a job like mine after a year or five years. It just doesn't work that way, and I think if people could come out of business schools with a more realistic sense of how things really operate in organizations, and know that there is a bit of dues-paying that has to happen, we'd all be better off."

Linda Hudson, the CEO of BAE Systems, said she too was struck by the impatience of many business school graduates.

"I find new business school graduates come in here thinking that, first of all, they're going to run the company overnight," Hudson said. "Many of them are convinced they've never made a mistake. They're not accustomed to encountering the kinds of roadblocks or disappointments that often come with the way decisions get made in a corporate environment, and they have almost no people skills.

"So I think an important part of teaching business ought to be focused more on realistic expectations and the people-skill part of business, dealing with failure, learning from adverse experiences, navigating the corporate environment. Because quite often they don't get it, and they have not been taught the coping skills of being told no, or being told that they can't have what it is they think they need. We give them all the book smarts, but we don't tend to give them the other skills that go along with business."

She said new employees should focus more on figuring out the culture of an organization.

"I tell people that in a corporate environment, which is all I've ever known, first and foremost you need to understand the culture you work in, and find a way to make it work for you rather than trying to fight it," Hudson said. "Corporations are very interesting machines. And what you need to look for is the informal power of the corporation, not necessarily the way the organization looks. An early boss told me, 'Spend the first couple of months in this job figuring out how things really work around here, and then go and establish alliances with the real movers and shakers in the organization because that's the way you will be the most successful.' And I advise people to do the same thing. You can never succeed in a corporate culture on your own. It is all about how you fit, how you know how to make things happen within the infrastructure and in a way that's acceptable to the norms and values of the corporation that you work in.

"Once you catch on to who really pulls the strings and where the real power base is, whom you have to collaborate with, whom you have to inform, whom you have to seek out for advice and agreement, you can actually make these big, very, very lumbering organizations work very, very well. It's all about the informal structure. It's about the critical relationships, and it's about fitting in, in a constructive way, so that you really make decisions that not only benefit yourself but benefit the corporation as well."

Everyone gets stuck with a bad boss once in a while—or maybe more often than that. Carol Bartz of Yahoo says it can be tempting to flee from them. But even in those situations, people should show patience, and try to make the most of the situation rather than act impulsively.

"I think people should understand that they will learn more

from a bad manager than a good manager," she said. "They tend to get into a cycle where they're so frustrated that they aren't actually paying attention to what's happening to them. When you have a good manager, things go so well that you don't even know why it's going well because it feels fine. When you have a bad manager you have to look at what's irritating you and say: 'Would I do that? Would I make those choices? Would I talk to me that way? How would I do this?'

"When people come to me and say, 'I can't work for so-and-so anymore,' I say, 'Well, what have you learned from so-and-so?' People want to take a bad situation and say, 'Oh, it's bad.' No, no. You have to deal with what you're dealt. Otherwise you're going to run *from* something and not *to* something. And you should never run from something."

Dawn Lepore of Drugstore.com also had an experience working for a bad boss, and from it she learned an important lesson about when to be patient, and when it's time to leave.

"I had a very bad boss early in my career," Lepore said. "She was older than I was. She'd started in the financial services industry and she'd had a very hard time, so I think that probably shaped her as a leader. She was very smart but had terrible communication skills. She did not make people feel valued or comfortable or like they were supported at all. And I remember what that felt like. And I thought, I'm never going to do that to people."

Lepore said she almost left twice during her many years of working for this boss, but she decided to stay.

"Life is about trade-offs," she said, summarizing her advice for others. "And you have to be conscious of the trade-off you're making. I felt there were enough other positives in the environment and enough opportunity that I stuck it out. But you know, I was unhappy. I had to just take a deep breath and say, 'Okay, I know this is going to end and I'm willing to put up with this.' But you can't be a victim. If you let yourself become a victim, that's the kiss of death. So you've got to feel, okay, I am choosing to do this, and when I decide I can no longer do it, then I will take action. So I will not let myself be so belittled that I think I can't do anything. If it starts undermining your confidence, then you have to leave, because then that seeps into everything you do."

Terry J. Lundgren, the CEO of Macy's, recounted a memorable story about when he learned about the value of patience in a career.

"I was moved into my first assistant buying job," Lundgren said. "The guy I was working for, I didn't love him, frankly, and he had me doing what I thought were stupid jobs. I was working hard, but I was literally handwriting transfers of furniture from one store to another store, and I wondered, 'Is this a really good use of my time, or is there something else I could do?' I happened to get called up by the guy who recruited me from campus, for whom I had total admiration, a guy named Gene Ross. And I told him, 'Well, it's not really going that great, and I was wondering, you know, if I could move to another department, I think I could do more.'

"And he just nodded his head and looked at me, and he pointed over his shoulder to a poster in his office. It had a little tree in a pot, and it said, 'Bloom where you're planted.' And I thought, 'Okay, I get it.' And he said, 'You're not going to do this forever. There's a finite amount of time you're going to be doing this. Do this really, really well. And if you do this really, really well, everybody will see that, and they'll move you on to the next thing. And you do that well, and then you'll move.' And that was fantastic advice for me."

Ursula Burns of Xerox offered an insightful lesson about careers and patience—something she heard from a previous boss, about the importance of "getting to zero." She explained it with the help of a piece of paper—she drew a line across the middle, and shaded an area below the left end of the line.

"When you start the job, whatever it is, you have to find out who the secretary is, where the bathrooms are, who your teammates are. Trust me, for a lot of time you are operating below zero," she said.

She pointed to the middle part of the line.

"This is when most people want to leave a job. They say, 'I'm done. I know everything. I'm done.' But think about that. If you left there, basically all this area under the curve, which is negative, which is takeaway, you owe the company all of that. Then you do this for six more months, and you can operate the place smoothly, but you haven't really transformed it in the ways that you can help to transform it."

She started shading an area above the line to the right. That represented what a manager is expected to contribute—give back—after absorbing all of the training and experience below the left side of the line. The net balance amounts to "getting to zero."

"You can only leave after you put in as much above the curve as under the curve," Burns said. "Unfortunately, that usually takes more than a day, and it takes a couple years. People would come in to me and say, 'You put me in this developmental assignment. I know how to run the place now. Thank you. Can I go to the next one?' I say, 'Well, how about all the stuff that you owe us? How about getting settled in for a little while longer and then start to transform it?'"

∾

Joseph Plumeri of Willis Group Holdings offered a useful piece of advice to underscore the importance of serendipity and relationships. His metaphor—playing in traffic—might make parents of young children cringe, but it's a memorable phrase to underscore how chance meetings can change the entire course of a career.

"Everything that I have done I've done because I went out and I played in traffic and something happened," he said. "If you push yourself out there and you see people and do things and partici-pate and get involved, something happens. I got involved with my first job at Cogan, Berlind, Weill & Levitt. It had four names, so I thought it was a law firm. I was going to law school. My last class was over at noon, and so I thought I'd go over to Wall Street and find a job in the afternoon with a law firm.

"So I go knock on doors and I see Cogan and I figure it's a law firm. So I go up to see the receptionist, and ask who could I see about a job? And she says go down the hall, make a left, and see Mr. Weill. I didn't know who Sandy Weill was. This was 1968. And he said what can I do for you? So I gave him the spiel about law school in the morning, learning the practical part in the after-noon. A really good pitch. And he says that's a great idea, but what makes you think you'll be learning law here? I said, this is a law firm. He said no, this is a brokerage firm. I tried to find the hole to climb into. I'm not easily embarrassed, and he laughed. He gave me a job working part-time. That firm turned into Citigroup.

"When I left Citigroup after all those years, I was walking down a street in Paris, and I ran into Henry Kravis by accident. He said what are you doing? I said I'm looking for my next adven-ture, because I'd just left Citigroup. And he said I've got this com-pany we just bought—Willis. I said what is it? He says it's an insurance broker. Two weeks later, he calls me. You know the rest of the story. So both of my great occasions in life happened by accident simply because I showed up. And I tell people, just show up, get in the game, go play in traffic. Something good will come of it, but you've got to show up."

Many CEOs echoed this advice. Take the time to meet people and to build relationships. They may help take you further, and faster, along the career obstacle course than a sense of impatience.

"Early in your career, find the time to do the out-of-the-norm," said Stephen Sadove of Saks. "Do whatever's required to do the job—run the budgets, execute the promotions. But you're never going to differentiate yourself just doing what everybody else can do. Find the time to build relationships outside of your own chain of command. I've been amazed over the years how relationships that come out of one thing go toward something else."

PART TWO

MANAGING

7.

THE SURPRISES THAT AWAIT YOU

A worker is promoted to a manager for the first time, with responsibilities for overseeing a small team of colleagues. Another has earned a promotion to lead a bigger department, and in this position she must manage other managers. A third has just been named by the board to be CEO, and he is packing up for a move to the corner office.

These are vastly different jobs, reflecting an enormous range of responsibilities. But they are similar in a key respect. Anyone new to them is likely to feel surprised, on a number of fronts: the intense scrutiny, the weight of responsibility, the amount of work, the challenge of managing new layers of people, and the way employees assume the boss has both superhuman knowledge and power.

As much as people can try to prepare for these jobs, they're likely to feel blindsided. That's a lesson many CEOs share, and their experiences are useful for managers at all levels, helping them to prepare for promotions into new roles, and to develop their sensitivity to the potential outsized impact of a small gesture or an offhand remark. Management jobs are a very public form of on-the-job training—people have to learn how to handle the work under the bright lights of center stage as employees scrutinize every move. The sooner executives appear comfortable in the role, the quicker they will win the confidence of employees.

The reality of management has a way of steamrolling the theory of management, particularly for anyone taking on such a role for the first time.

"When I was getting my education, I fell in love with the writings of Peter Drucker," said Guy Kawasaki of Alltop and Garage Technology Ventures. "He was my hero. I had a naïve belief that when I became a manager, it was going to be like Peter Drucker's books. That is, I was going to be the effective executive. I was going to talk to people about their goals. I was going to help them actualize. My thinking was: I'm a natural leader, so I'm going to study what's hard and mathematical like finance and operations research, not the touchy-feely stuff that would be easy.

"When I finally got a management position, I found out how hard it is to lead and manage people. The warm, fuzzy stuff is hard. The quantitative stuff is easy—you either don't do much of this as a manager or you have people working for you to do it. Maybe it was just my education, but much of education is backwards. You study all the hard stuff, and then you find out in the real world that you don't use it. As long as you can use an HP-12 calculator or a spreadsheet, you have the finance knowledge you need for most management positions. I should have taken organizational behavior and social psychology—and maybe abnormal psychology, come to think of it."

The surprises keep coming throughout management. Another big one arrives for people who take on the top role.

Lawrence W. Kellner had been the number two at Continental Airlines, and had a front-row seat watching Gordon Bethune run the carrier for several years. It was an opportunity to develop a keen sense of what the job would entail come the day he would take over. He didn't expect to be surprised by much when he was named CEO in 2004. He was wrong.

"What surprised me was how different it is when it is ultimately your decision," he recalled. "You may not make every decision, but it's ultimately your decision. So it's a little bit like being a parent. People can describe being a parent to you and you think you know what it's going to be like to be a parent. And then you become a parent and you say, 'Wow.' I think there are life events that are difficult to understand until you've done them. Taking the top job is one of those events. I wouldn't have thought that before I did it, but it clearly fit in that group of things where you say, 'Okay, this is hard to describe to people.' It's not quite what you anticipated—how many people are looking for your time, and all the responsibilities and the demands."

Several executives spoke of moments when they realized they were truly in charge. No longer could they get others to sign off on their work. Susan Lyne of Gilt Groupe shared a story from her days working at a magazine:

"When I was first editing *Premiere* magazine, it was the first time I had ever been the number-one leader. I had always been managing editor before that, so there was a person I could go to and say, 'This is what I think we should do.' We had our first issue coming out, and my instinct was to go to my boss, who was John Evans, a very interesting guy who was running Murdoch Magazines at the time and was a longtime mentor to me, even after I left there. And I sent him my 'editor's letter,' because I was thinking, 'Let me get some feedback here.' And he called me up, and he said, 'What is this?' And I said, 'It's my editor's letter. I just thought you'd like to see it.' He said, 'I don't buy a dog and bark for it. Don't ever send me your editor's letter again.' I took away from it that, okay, I'm going to live and die by my own success here, and I'm not going to get away with being the number two anymore. So I'd better get comfortable with my decisions, my voice."

The sheer weight of responsibility can also be surprising. William Green of Accenture talked about how he felt when he was elevated to the top role.

"The amount of responsibility you carry around on your back is unbelievable," he said. "It's not like you're a martyr—it just comes with the territory. There's something going on around the globe in our place 24/7, and the sense of responsibility you feel for all those people and their families is profound. I like taking the responsibility, but I had no idea about the spiritual part. The spiritual obligation to the lives of 177,000 people is a big deal. I'm a guy who had trouble being responsible for his own life in the early days, and now I've got 177,000 people that look up to me. That took a little getting used to."

～

All eyes are on you. Every shrug of your shoulders, every stern look, even the way you walk—are you confident and energetic, or do you seem weighed down?—will be subjected to obsessive scrutiny for clues by your employees.

Linda Hudson of BAE Systems remembers the moment she realized how intensely she was being watched when she moved into the corner office.

"It was when I first became a company president," she said. "I had moved up progressively through organizations over the years with increasing responsibilities, but it was the first time I found myself in a job where I truly was the one who was responsible for the performance of a company. I had mastered the day-to-day mechanics of running organizations, if you will. But I don't think the leadership part of it had settled in quite as profoundly as it did when I took over a company.

"And it may sound a bit trivial, but for me it was profound. I had just been promoted to become the first female president at General Dynamics, and I went out and bought my new fancy suits to wear to work. A lady at Nordstrom had showed me how to tie a scarf in a very unusual kind of way for my new suit. I go to work the next day and wear my suit. And then I come back to work the next day, and I run into no fewer than a dozen women in the organization wearing scarves tied exactly like mine.

"And that's when I realized that life was never going to be the way it had been before, that people were watching everything I did. And it wasn't just going to be about how I dressed. It was about my behavior, the example I set, the tone I set, the way I carried myself, how confident I was—all those kinds of things. It really was now about me and the context of setting the tone for the organization. And that was a lesson I have never forgotten—as the leader, people are looking at you in a way you could not have imagined in other roles. And I didn't see that nearly as profoundly when I was leading a functional organization or a smaller enterprise. But to this day, not only the awareness of that, but the responsibility that goes along with it, is something I think about virtually every day."

Deborah Dunsire, the CEO of Millennium, a pharmaceutical company, said that she learned to appreciate the power of the CEO title. She recalled that an HR executive once advised her, "What you have to think about now that you're in this position is that you have this megaphone attached to your shoulder that amplifies everything you do."

She explained how she came to appreciate this insight.

"As I was transitioning into more senior leadership levels, people would take their cues by what I looked like," she said. "So if I looked really concerned and worried, which I sometimes do if I'm thinking deeply about something, and somebody would say hello to me and ask how I am, I'd say, 'Oh, fine, thanks,' and keep moving. That, as a senior leader, communicates far more than you ever intended it to. It just meant to me that I've got something else on my mind right now. But the feedback I got was that sometimes the organization will take away from your demeanor a message that you don't realize and might not be what you intended.

"So I learned to engage more when people ask me how I am. I'll be very authentic, because I do think you need to be always authentic. People will ask me how I am, and I'll say, 'I'm great and here's why.' And I'll tell them about why things are going great in the business. Or if there's a revenue decline or something we're not expecting, I'll talk about the challenge and here's how we're going to face it. Those thoughts are always in my head, but I've learned to be more outspoken with them so that people don't assume how you're feeling or thinking. They make inferences about how the business is going, their job security, whether they should accept a call from a recruiter, and that's a very quick leap for a person. You don't want your talent thinking that either you're not interested in them, you're angry with them or the business is going badly and they need to go work somewhere else because you simply didn't take the time to communicate effectively what was actually going on in your mind. So I think I've learned to overcommunicate in a way I never did before."

Clarence Otis of Darden Restaurants said his awareness of the scrutiny of the chief executive made him more sensitive to the words he uses at work.

"I would say it's amplified everything that you say or do," he said. "That was the case at every senior job. It's even more true of this position. And so, you have to be very intentional about what you say and do. If you're not, then something that was just thinking out loud, some thought you had, some 'what if' becomes a directive, even though ten seconds later in your own mind you dismissed it."

Many CEOs said they had learned the importance of presenting a consistent demeanor at the office so that employees are not confused or distracted by having to decipher the signals they send to people around them.

"I never fully appreciated that there are people who choose certain things in life where they can't have a bad day," said Joseph Plumeri of Willis Group Holdings. "I can't have a bad day. If I walk into a meeting and I'm grumpy—not good. There are certain professions you choose where you can't have a bad day. My doctor can't have a bad day. And I think anybody in a leadership position where people depend upon you has to simply realize that you can't have that one off-day, because you're going to affect a lot of people."

Jeffrey Swartz, the CEO of Timberland, a company founded by his family, said he learned an important lesson from his father about consistency in managing people.

"My dad told me when I first went to work for him as a little kid, 'No one cares,'" Swartz recalled. "And I said, 'What do you mean?' He said, 'If you had a bad night last night, that's your problem. Pick a face.' I remember him saying this: 'Pick a face. If you want to be serious, then you have to be serious all the time. Because if you're serious one day and happy the next day, people will be confused. They won't be able to figure out where you're coming from, and that'll be threatening.'"

Jilly Stephens of City Harvest said she learned to be open with employees so that they are not left wondering what's on her mind.

"It's important that you communicate clearly with people who are going to be reporting to you, that you be as open as possible about who you are, what they should know about you, what they should understand about you, and how you like to operate," she said. "I remember learning that very early on in my own career—having to sit and think about what I needed to let people know about me. I even said to people that I've been told that I look angry a lot of the time, and I'm usually not. It's just my face, so just don't be put off by that. Again, just be very clear about what you expect of the people who are going to be reporting to you."

∾

Drew Gilpin Faust, the president of Harvard University, said she was struck by how people assumed she had far more power and knowledge than she actually had.

"One thing I learned was that people impute all kinds of things to leaders," she said. "Sometimes it's thinking of them as hugely powerful and imagining them to be much more transcendently significant in what they can accomplish, and to have many more tools and weapons than they actually do. Another is to imagine that they have all kinds of designs or purposes that they may or may not have. So communication seemed to me something very important from early on, so that people not have that sense of mystery about what a leader is up to, in that sense of possible misunderstandings.

"I remember being told by members of the department that it was clear that I was out to hire so-and-so, who had been my student. And it never occurred to me to hire that person. I wondered what I'd done to make it seem to them so clearly that I had this design, when I had no such design at all."

To hear these CEOs describe their lives, there are moments when they probably feel like movie stars, given how hard it can be to go out in public without someone approaching them. That's not necessarily true in cities like Manhattan, where celebrities can easily get lost in the crowds. But in smaller cities and towns where everybody knows you, the attention can be exhausting.

Daniel P. Amos, the CEO of Aflac, the insurance company, shared his experiences working and living in Columbus, Georgia, where his company is headquartered. He said he has had to adjust to the realities, for better and worse, of the CEO title.

"You have to be careful, or you'll become aloof," he said. "But I'm always amazed that everywhere you go, people want something from you. 'My daughter needs a job.' 'My son needs a consulting contract.' Whatever it is. So that brings on the aloofness or the loneliness. But you just have to work through that, or otherwise you'll end up being withdrawn to some degree, and I think that's the biggest mistake you can make. You have to accept it for what it is and go on."

When Nancy McKinstry became CEO of Wolters Kluwer, she had a couple of surprises about the degree of scrutiny she would face in the chief executive's role. One of them is an important lesson in how the scrutiny can be used to send an important signal about the culture a CEO tries to create.

First, the disappointment. "Everything you do is evaluated," she said. "I remember doing some meeting about our strategy, and the press in Holland wrote that I wore a suit that had the same color as the KLM flight attendants, which I didn't realize when I bought the suit. I remember thinking, 'Here we were talking about the plans for the business and that's what they focused on.'"

But then came an instance where the scrutiny helped, unintentionally, to send a positive message to employees.

"People watch little things," she said. "I have two children, and as part of my expat arrangement, my children get to fly back to the United States twice a year, and they're allowed to fly business class. I said, 'No, they're going to fly coach.' I remember somebody from the HR department coming to me and saying, 'Everybody really likes it that you make your kids fly coach.' And I said, 'Well, how do they even know?' It was the people in accounts payable. I think people have this image that CEOs kind of live high on the hog, and I said, 'No, of course they can fly coach.' But it was remarkable that people kept mentioning that to me within the company. You realize that what they were really saying is, 'We like the fact that you're one of us and that you're going to sacrifice as much as you're going to ask me to sacrifice.' In the end, that's what it really meant to me."

There are other positive surprises that await the top boss.

"I've been surprised by how people put the CEO on such a high pedestal, and that you get more credit than you deserve for being friendly and approachable," said David Novak of Yum Brands. "I've never been able to understand that, but it's true. If you treat everybody like they should be treated, there's a high degree of appreciation for that."

8.

TIME MANAGEMENT

Few people face greater time-management challenges than CEOs. After all, as their title implies, they are ultimately in charge of everything, and the demands are relentless and seemingly unlimited—from the board, employees, customers, management committees. The list goes on.

How to handle it all?

Certainly one answer is to sleep less. Anybody who can get by on minimal sleep can get a huge leg up. And a number of CEOs said they can get by on very little rest.

Jeffrey Katzenberg, the CEO of DreamWorks Animation, said he's never needed more than five hours of sleep a night since he was a teenager. He said it's one of his three greatest assets, and they're all genetic. (The other two are that he can fall asleep on command, wherever he is, and that he never feels jet lag.)

"For 99.999 percent of the people on the planet, they actually have a seven-day week," Katzenberg said. "I have an eight-day week. I literally get an extra day a week. That's a big advantage."

But even for those who can get by on less sleep, the challenge remains the same for everyone who stares up at a mountain of tasks and wonders how they're going to get it all done.

Many CEOs have developed frameworks for establishing priorities, for themselves and their organizations, that offer useful lessons about how to be more effective in any job. Time management is an increasingly valuable skill as the workload of every job seems to grow, and the endless distractions of e-mails and buzzing Black-Berrys make it harder to stay focused. Global businesses require conference calls early in the morning or late at night. Clients expect answers right away, whatever the hour. It's very easy to get pulled into a multitasking mania.

So what is their advice?

David Novak of Yum Brands said that an effective check on how you're spending your time is to ask yourself whether what you're doing is "action" or "activity."

"A lot of times there are certain things you do almost out of ritual, like creating a report that everybody looks at," Novak explained. "But when you really step away from it, it's more activity than action. What I've learned is to make sure I spend time on the action that's going to drive results. I've worked very hard to get my calendar filled with things that will really move the needle versus activity that might make you feel good. I think experience gives you the ability to put more process and discipline around what really matters in your business. You get much better at homing in on the things that really count.

"Let's take something that everybody does. Everybody has a BlackBerry. Everybody has e-mail. So you can really feel good going through all these e-mails and getting your e-mails wiped out, but the reality is that you haven't really taken the business that much further. So that activity, the fact that you were able to clean out all your e-mails, might make you feel good, but did it really grow the business? Probably not. That's just one small example. I remember one situation where every Monday everybody reviewed the market performance over the weekend, market by market. Meanwhile, the business overall was not doing that well. So people were just reporting how the business was doing versus figuring out the actions it would take to fix the business. I think leadership is all around driving the actions that keep you growing. One of the things you have to worry about as a leader is to make sure that you're not just creating activity. I'm very careful about what reports I ask for. It might be nice to know, but do I really need to know it? And 'nice to know' information is activity. 'Need to know' information leads to action."

Lawrence Kellner, CEO of Continental Airlines, said he learned to manage his time better by constantly assessing and reassessing his top priorities. Once he learned how to do that for himself, he then used that system to help establish priorities for the whole company.

"I used to have a long, long to-do list, and I've always managed my life and managed time by using a to-do list," Kellner said. "At the end of the day, I'd click through and see which ones got done and mark them off. Then five more notes might be on my desk, and, as I'm cleaning up for the day, I'd throw them on the list. At some point I realized that a lot of times I was doing what came to me as opposed to what was really important. So I started coming to work and saying, 'Okay, what are the three most important things I need to do today?' And I'm going to rank them one-two-three. And if number one is a twelve-hour task, then I'll just spend all day working on it. I need to decide what's the most value-added thing that I can get done on this list.

"As I moved further up in management, my calendar started getting kind of messy. So I sat down and said, 'Okay, I've got 250 workdays,' or whatever it was. 'How many will I spend on Wall Street? How many will I spend on Washington? How many will I spend doing sales calls with the sales team?' And then I went to the head of each department and gave them a budget of X number of days of my time, and told them, 'Okay, you get X. You've got your budget. If I'm free, you can use it. But that's all you get.'

"And then, the last piece I came to, when I became CEO, was to end each of my three most important meetings each month by saying, 'Okay, here are the three most important things we're doing. Here are the three priorities.' What I found very early was if I put something on the list of three, I was amazed at the amount of resources that would be applied to getting that done, because nobody liked being in the top three. But at the same time, I had to be really careful to pick the things that were going to create the most value."

Mark Pincus of Zynga adopted a system called OKRs—which stands for "objectives and key results"—to manage his time. Like Kellner, he then applied his personal system to the whole organization.

"John Doerr [the venture capitalist] sold me on this idea of OKRs," he said. "It was developed at Intel and used at Google, and the idea is that the whole company and every group has one objective and three measurable key results, and if you achieve two of the three, you achieve your overall objective, and if you achieve all three, you've really killed it. And we put the whole company on that, so everyone knows their OKRs. And that is a good simple organizing principle that keeps people focused on the three things that matter—not the ten.

"Then I ask everybody to write down on Sunday night or Monday morning what your three priorities are for the week, and then on Friday see how you did against them. It's the only way people can stay focused and not burn out. And if I look at your road map and you have ten priorities for you and your team, you probably don't know which of the ten matter, and probably none of the ten is right.

"I can look at everyone's piece of paper, and each road map shows every item you were going to do and your predicted results and actual results, and then the results are in red if you missed them, yellow if they're close, and green if you passed them. I think road maps are a great principle for managing your life. It keeps everybody focused, and it lets me know what trains are on or off the tracks."

Alan Mulally of the Ford Motor Company said he manages his time by focusing on four key aspects of his job, then letting his schedule flow from those priorities.

"I pay attention to everything, but there are some things that are unique to what I need to do as the leader," Mulally said. "I have to really come through on these. And one of them is this process of connecting what we're doing to the outside world. I mean, we're here to create a business of serving customers with the best cars and trucks in the world, so where is the world going? Where is the technology going? Where are the customers going? Where is the competition going?

"A second focus for me is: What business are we in? What are we going to focus on? What's going to be our business? Are we going to have a house of brands of vehicles? Are we going to focus on the blue oval [the company logo]? Are we going to be competitive on quality and cost and fuel efficiency? Are we going to be best in class? So what's our point of view about the value proposition of our company?

"The third one that I really focus on is balancing the near term with the longer term—and especially in the environment we see today, where you absolutely want to keep investing for the future, even though you could invest less and make your business performance look better in the near term. Do we have a plan that works in the near term and also creates value for the long term?

"And then I really focus on the values and the standards of the organization. What are the expected behaviors? How do we want to treat each other? How do we want to act? What do we want to do about transparency? How can we have a safe environment where we really know what's going on?

"I'm the one who needs to focus on those four things, because if I do that, the entire team will have a collective point of view and an understanding of all four of those areas. I look at those four priorities, and I look at the process every week, and then I just decide—is that what I need to do? Our most important asset is our time, because whatever we spend time on is what is going to get addressed."

One of the most consistent messages to emerge from discussions with CEOs on time management is the notion that, even amid all the chaos, people should make time—daily, weekly, or quarterly—to study their time and to assess and analyze how they're using it.

Wendy Kopp of Teach for America said that just ten minutes a day can make a big difference.

"The best time-management thing I do is reflect an hour a

week on the overall strategic plan for myself—what do I need to do to move my priorities forward?" she said. "And then there are the ten minutes a day I spend thinking about, 'Okay, so based on the priorities for the week, how am I going to prioritize my day tomorrow?' I don't know how I could do what I do without spending that time. I am obsessive about that system because the world seems to be moving faster and faster, so you have to figure out how to drive things proactively instead of just becoming completely reactive."

Susan Lyne of Gilt Groupe also sets aside time to step back and think about her highest priorities for setting the direction of the company.

"One of the things I do is make sure I can carve out a certain period of time every week to step back and think about the big picture," she said. "Early in my career, I was constantly looking at what was coming next week, next month, but I rarely carved out time to really think about what we were shooting for. It's useful on so many levels, not just because it gives you long-term focus, but because it forces you to reassess all those short-term decisions, too. I need time alone, quiet time alone, to do my job well. It's usually either six o'clock to eight o'clock in the morning, or it's a weekend afternoon. It's never in the office. It's my apartment, my library, and I usually have multiple pieces of paper on a big table in front of me that I can always access if I need them. But a lot of it is just a notebook and a pencil. That's it."

Cristóbal Conde of SunGard said he builds thinking time into his daily schedule.

"I tell my secretary, 'Once a day, I need an hour and a half where I can go somewhere that doesn't have a PC or a phone,' unless I choose to spend that hour and a half writing," he said.

"But it's not just managing e-mails and things like that. I need an hour and a half to think. And it could be anything. But there are many times where you need solid focus. So I've learned that it's incredibly useful to reserve some time. And then she moves that time slot around according to what else is going on that day. Sometimes it gets cut short. Sometimes things happen. But it's the realization that many topics or issues can only be dealt with in an uninterrupted format. I worry about our entry-level people—they're bombarded with all these BlackBerrys and everything else, and they never get to think. They feel that they must reply immediately."

Certainly one way to get away from all the gadgets is to go to a place where they not only don't work, but they're also banned: at 35,000 feet or so on a plane—and, ideally, a corporate jet to really get that quiet time. Although the travel schedule of CEOs can be grueling, flying time is, they admit, a useful opportunity to think in peace and quiet.

"Most people in my position would say that as much as we'll whine about traveling, time on planes probably is critically important to us doing our jobs," said Anne Mulcahy, the former Xerox CEO. "It's time to be reflective. It's time to catch up. It's time to really be thoughtful and communicate. So I get off a plane with just a ton done, and that's really important in terms of time management."

Many executives make time for themselves away from their gadgets. Dany Levy of DailyCandy.com explained her lunchtime routine.

"There are tugs every second of every moment, and there's a dearth of white space, that downtime," she said. "I have gotten better about not checking my e-mail as incessantly, simply because I felt like everything I was doing was just a reaction to something.

In terms of creativity, that allowed me no time to actually come up with anything new, because I was constantly just reacting.

"I'm a big runner and when I run it's as close to meditation as it gets, I think. It's the one thing that I'm compulsive about. The office basically knows that usually at lunchtime I'm on the treadmill. I often make to-do lists on the treadmill. But that's good white space for me. I also try to keep my home office very white and simple. And my bedroom—I declared it a media-free zone, because you just have to turn it off at some point."

Gary McCullough of Career Education Corporation turns off his BlackBerry at the end of the week so others on his staff will, too.

"I live by my BlackBerry, as most of us do," he said. "I do make it a point on Friday night to turn it off, and I don't turn it on again until Sunday morning. I do that for a couple of reasons. One is, you have to try to separate at some point during the week. Anybody who needs me, whether it's a board member or one of my leaders, knows how to reach me if something comes up that's a crisis. The other reason I turn it off is because when things come in, if I respond, then I've got people in the organization who would see that I've responded on Saturday morning at eight a.m. And the next thing I know, I have a response to my response at eight-fifteen and so it goes. And I want people to have a life."

Back at the office, McCullough has an interesting strategy for making sure his one-on-one meetings are to the point. Whenever somebody at Career Education Corporation calls his office to request a meeting, his assistant asks the person to explain the reason for the meeting and how much time is needed. If she agrees that McCullough should take the meeting, she will then allot them half the time that was requested.

"People rarely need as much time as they believe they need if we're clear and concise and stay on point," McCullough said. "And so, in doing that, I'm able to cram a number of things into the day and move people in and out more effectively and more efficiently. If we took every meeting and if we spent all the hours that people ask for, I wouldn't sleep very much, brush my teeth here and change my clothes, and do it again. There's not enough time in the day."

9.

BANANAS, BELLS, AND THE ART OF RUNNING MEETINGS

Everybody's been stuck in a bad meeting at one time or another. Some people, in fact, find themselves stuck in a bad meeting on a daily basis.

We've all suffered and fidgeted and daydreamed through them, checking our watches, wondering when they would end. The goals aren't clear. Two people are having a conversation that's not relevant to the other ten people in the room. Somebody filibusters. Another person shows off for the boss. Somebody criticizes everyone else's ideas to make himself look smarter, but he contributes nothing himself. Sometimes, it's not even clear why you're meeting—other than that you've always met at this time each week or each month. People are checking their BlackBerrys. The meeting ends with little or no resolution. You walk out of the room muttering to yourself, "Well, that was a waste of time."

Some of the solutions to meeting-malaise are obvious. Having a clear agenda and sticking to a timetable certainly helps.

But many CEOs have developed a smart set of tools and tricks to elevate the quality of meetings, and to handle some of the trickier situations and tense moments that can arise.

The goals in each case are to keep people fully engaged, and to set clear rules about expectations of behavior so that the group knows when a line is crossed. Meetings have developed a bad reputation, which is unfortunate. It's worth figuring out how to crack the code of how to run an effective meeting. If you can get the sparks flying, harness the collective brain power, and get a free flow of ideas going, the results can be remarkable. If you think of meetings as a sport—and assume your competitors are meeting at the same time you do—then it will help focus the group on finding ways to get the most out of the time spent together. The point of the meeting is to drive progress, however that is measured.

Cristóbal Conde of SunGard has a simple rule to stay focused on moving ahead, rather than wasting time: "The question from the beginning of the meeting to the end of the meeting is, 'Have we added value: yes or no?'"

Why Are We Here?

People will be more engaged if they're clear about the point of the meeting from the start. They will also appreciate it if the person leading the meeting makes the point clear to all, to keep the discussion on track. What's the goal? Are the right people in the room?

"I like to be very, very clear at the beginning of the meeting— this is what we're going to accomplish before the end of the meeting," said Nell Minow of The Corporate Library. "People have agendas other than achieving that one goal for that meeting, and so you've just got to keep bringing people back to that. People I work with know I don't like meetings and that they will do better to just keep it moving."

William Green of Accenture established a couple of useful rules for keeping meetings focused for his leadership group.

"One is that half of the meeting is focused on the outside world, as opposed to the inside world," he said. "Too many leadership meetings are all focused on internals, so half of the meeting has to be externally facing—our market share, our clients, our service, what we're doing, and I'm religious about that. In fact, we keep track of the topics. The second thing is that we come up with the actions on the day of the meeting, and who is committed to doing them, because so many meetings are just a frightening waste of time. What is the thing we're trying to get done? What is the action that comes out of it and who is responsible for it? How do we put it in their hot little hands in a public way at the end of the discussion? I think we've got a never-ending journey to make meetings more effective."

Teresa Taylor of Qwest Communications said that sometimes, particularly with groups of colleagues who don't report to her directly, she will begin a meeting by going around the table and having everyone explain why they think they are there.

"So many people say, 'No, I don't know, I was invited,'" she said. "It's usually the bigger meetings—not so much my direct-report team. I get invited to a lot of meetings where someone wants to brief me, or bring me up to speed on something, which usually means that they want to tell me about their project and then ask me for money. So I open with, 'Do we all know why we're here? Are we making decisions? Are you going to ask me for something at the end?' I try to get that out right away. It's amazing, there will be eight people in the room and they all have a different answer of what's going on there. It gives me a way to make sure we're all together, and if we are, great. If not, if there's a disconnect, then you can correct that really quickly. I'll also say, once we're clear about what we're doing, 'Does everyone need to be here? If anyone feels like they want to leave right now, that would be fine.' Every once in a while a couple of people will say, 'Yeah, I could use this time back,' and they get up and leave."

Will Wright, the video-game developer, said he even encourages people to speak up at meetings if they feel that the gathering isn't a good use of their time. What might be an otherwise awkward moment becomes instead a signal about staying focused.

"We would invite one of my lead artists, a guy named Ocean Quigley, to these general creative meetings," Wright said. "He gets very impatient when things go off track and are not relevant to him, and I found that Ocean was like the canary in the coal mine. Whenever the meeting started getting off track, Ocean would usually raise his hand and say something like, 'Oh, do you need me in the meeting anymore?' And then he would try to get out of the meeting. And so that was the point at which we always knew the meeting had hit diminishing returns, because our canary had put up his hand. It's more of a philosophy we try to convey to everybody on the team. It's almost more like you want to encourage everybody to be a hall monitor. 'Hey, are we wasting our time here, or not?' We try to give positive feedback: 'Oh, you're right, you know, we're wasting time here. You five can leave.' Not making it taboo is the main thing. It is purely a cost-benefit issue, right? It's nothing personal."

Who should be in the meeting? Will Wright encourages people to leave if they don't feel they have anything to add, but others take a different tack. Kip Tindell, the CEO of The Container Store, said that executives at his company meet frequently, and often bring more people into the discussion to get their perspective, even if it's not immediately clear what they may be able to contribute.

"We're big on what we call the whole-brain concept, which is simply trying to eliminate silos," he said. "So we probably have more people than we need in each meeting, and we don't believe that's unproductive. In fact, we think it creates a whole-brain awareness. We get a lot of innovation that way. There's a real belief in meetings on our part. They're passionate. They're long. They're frequent. We get tired of being in meetings all the time. I know the whole world feels that way, but I actually think we're at meetings more than just about any other business I can think of. I think it's really good for us because of the communicative culture we have. Also, probably 85 percent of our top leaders are women. I don't want to get into a generalization here, but guess who tends to communicate the best? So I think there's a natural tendency for more group communication here than there would be if 85 percent of our top leaders were men."

Clear Rules

People like rules in meetings, and they like them even more when the rules are enforced fairly. That keeps everybody on track. When does a vigorous debate step over the line and become personal? If you want to encourage a level of candor, how do you make sure that whatever is said stays within the meeting?

Richard Anderson, the CEO of Delta Air Lines, uses a bell to defuse any tension that might arise. "Let's have a really good debate, but it can't get uncollegial," he said. "If it gets uncollegial, we actually have a bell you can ring, in the conference room. If you are in a really hard debate and somebody veers off the subject and goes after you in a way that isn't fair, you get to ring the bell. It's a violation of the rules of the road. So you ring the bell if something wasn't a fair shot, and we all laugh."

Many CEOs describe their meetings using a variety of metaphors. "We tend to run meetings a bit like a food fight here," said Greg Brenneman of CCMP. "Anybody can have an idea or a thought, and the best idea wins. And so there's not a lot of formality or pomp and circumstance around it, at all. It's a very informal and very free-flowing dialogue."

Or meetings can be like baseball: "The flow of information is good and it's fast," said Kevin Sharer, the CEO of Amgen. "It's sort of like being in the infield in a baseball game—the ball whips around the infield really fast, and the team can keep up. I think being succinct and efficient is also a measure of preparation and command of the facts."

If there are any disagreements, they are settled within the meeting, many CEOs insist—and there's no second-guessing afterward.

"I think it can be a little jarring, actually, for people who are used to perhaps a little more civility," said Barbara Krumsiek of the Calvert Group. "I think we're civil, but we're direct. I don't like meetings if my direct reports leave the room and turn to somebody and say, 'Can you believe someone said that?' And so I try to explain to them by example that if you find yourself doing that when you leave the room, or shaking your head, or kicking yourself for not having said something, or thinking that there were real problems with what somebody said, next time you have to say it in the room. You have to, or you will not be the most impactful member of this team."

Jacqueline Kosecoff, the CEO of Prescription Solutions, has a similar rule. "Silence is consent," she said. "If you don't speak up in the meeting, you can't later come back and say: 'I really hated that. I don't want it to happen.' Come to the meeting, let your feelings be heard, and a decision will be made."

Meetings, even at companies that are good at running them, can get bogged down. It can be useful to have a handy—and most important, consistent—way to signal to the team that it needs to pick up the pace or move on.

Anne Mulcahy, the former Xerox CEO, had a signature way to signal that the speed of the meeting was too slow for her.

"I'm not formal and I'm impatient," she said. "And I think my team would say that when she starts tapping her pen and the leg starts moving at a quick speed, that it's time to move on. I'm not good at long, drawn-out kinds of sessions, and therefore I want to get to the point. I want to not waste time. I want it to be something that we really need to be talking about, and it belongs at the table, if you will. So I would probably describe it as informal in the sense that you roll up your sleeves, it's a working session, and impatient because there's just not a lot of tolerance for something that's not decisionable or meaningful for the senior team. The tapping of the pen— absolutely, when that starts you know things are not going well."

Dawn Lepore of Drugstore.com uses a shorthand for signaling in meetings whether something she mentions is a passing thought for brainstorming or a directive.

"We have a little joke where I'll tell people, a lightbulb or a gun," she said. "A lightbulb means this is just an idea I had, so think about it, see if you think it's a good one. Either follow up or don't, but it's just an idea. A gun is, I want you to do this. People don't always know if you mean something as just as an idea, or you want them to go do it."

Sheila Lirio Marcelo, the CEO of Care.com, lets her staff know what kind of meeting it is with a shorthand for three different kinds of decisions that will be made.

"We do Type 1, Type 2, Type 3 decisions," she said. "Type 1 decisions are the decision-maker's sole decision—dictatorial. Type 2: people can provide input, and then the person can still make the decision. Type 3, it's consensus. It's a great way to efficiently solve a problem."

Involve Everyone

Meetings can easily descend into a conversation between two people, with others watching. Or they can run into that familiar problem where everyone is watching the CEO for her reaction to everything. How to combat that?

Jacqueline Kosecoff of Prescription Solutions says she often doesn't lead meetings. Instead, she has others do it.

"Every Friday, we have the senior leadership team come for about an hour-and-a-half operations check, and we have the checklist of items we need to get to, and we will go through that list, but I will never lead that meeting," she said. "Each one of the executives leads the meeting—it rotates in alphabetical order and we go through the list. First of all, it teaches them how to lead a meeting. It also sends a message that this meeting's not for me, it's for us. And it's been my observation that at a lot of these operations meetings, everyone talks to the CEO, not to each other. It also teaches good meeting etiquette. People are much more, I think, respectful of how they behave in a meeting because they're going to be leading the meeting one day."

Susan Docherty, a vice president at General Motors, said she's a fan of using a big whiteboard as a way to get everyone in a meeting involved.

"I love to brainstorm with my team around the table in my office," she said. "I like to use a big whiteboard for ideas, because when you make things visual, you encourage the team to get up there at the whiteboard and put their thoughts out there. It's one thing to say that you're inclusive, but it's a whole other thing to be inclusive. And when people come into my office, they feel welcome. My door is open. They can bring ideas. They begin to understand that, as a leader, I want to be collaborative. I don't have all the answers or all the best ideas, nor do I want to.

"The whiteboard also keeps great ideas in front of us, not buried in an e-mail and not buried in a stack of papers on our desks. And it enables everybody to own what we've got to get done. People will grab a marker and put up there that we're going to do a deep dive to figure something out, and they put their name beside it. And there are lots of times where we put something on the board, and it requires a couple of people to get together to go work on it."

Docherty also said she doesn't like assigned seats in a meeting room.

"I always sit in a different chair," she said. "When I was in different roles in this company, I saw a lot of leaders sit in the same chair, think the same way and talk to the same people. And I said to myself, 'When I become a leader, and I have a big team, I'm not going to play favorites. I want to be a dynamic leader.' And I think being disruptive, not always being predictable, is healthy."

Waiting for people to contribute doesn't always work. Sometimes you have to seek out opinions. CEOs said they make it a point to hold back on sharing what they think until they get more input.

"I tend to be a stoic going into the meeting," said Richard Anderson of Delta Air Lines. "I want the debate. I want to hear everybody's perspective, so you want to try to ask more questions than to make statements."

Robert W. Selander, the CEO of MasterCard, said he had learned over time to encourage discussion in a group.

"From sort of a style standpoint, I prefer to do what I call more of a consensus style of decision-making," he said. "So when I'm around the table with our executive committee, the senior leadership of the company, I could easily make a bilateral decision. You're knowledgeable about your area. I may have the best knowledge about your area or second best around the table. You and I agree. Let's get on with it. What we haven't done is we haven't benefited from the wisdom, the insight, and the experience of the others around the table. And while they may not have as much insight or knowledge about your area as you do, there's a chance that we missed something. So I try to get more engagement and discussion around topics and avoid what I would call bilateralism. I think what happens is sometimes you get an insight that's startling and important and affects the decision, but you also get participative involvement so that there is buy-in and a recognition of how we got to that decision. It's not as if the boss went off in a corner and waved a magic wand and, bang, out came the decision."

He's also learned to hold back on expressing his opinion.

"As you become more senior in a company, you tend to be viewed as more authoritative when you speak and therefore you have to back off a little bit," he said. "Otherwise you suppress, even though you don't intend to, the conversation by jumping in a little bit too early with your view or your perspective. No matter how you couch it, everybody sort of goes, 'Okay, this is the way the boss wants to go,' and you risk losing the engagement and that participation that you're looking for. So one of the things that I have found to be a challenge, because I tend to want to jump in and I tend to have that sort of control aspect, is sitting back and letting things percolate, and if we're not hearing from a couple of colleagues, you know, inviting them in. 'Do you have a perspective on that? Didn't you have a similar circumstance in this market a few years ago? How did you guys deal with that?' Whatever it may be to invite that participation. So better listening skills have been something that I've had to consciously focus on, because my colleagues have told me, 'You can shut things down real fast, even though you may not want to.'"

Dan Rosensweig, the CEO of Chegg, which rents textbooks, said his best strategy for getting everyone involved is to have a no-gadgets rule during meetings.

"It's so easy to get distracted in the world of BlackBerrys, iPhones, Twitter, Facebook, and five hundred e-mails a day," he said. "So with our management team, when we're in a meeting it starts on time, it ends on time, no technology. It's just, let's stay focused, and we have a much more healthy conversation. People really listen and contribute and we move on. It works well in your personal life as well—wherever you are, be all in."

Keep It Light

If meetings are fun rather than a slog through an agenda, people will be more engaged and listen to the rest of the group more intently. Some CEOs have found ways to keep them upbeat.

To set a light tone at the start of meetings—and maybe also to warm people up to the idea that they could learn something—Tony Hsieh, the CEO of Zappos, the online shoe retailer, will sometimes go around the table and ask people to share a random "fun fact." Many of them have laptops open during the meeting so they can quickly look one up.

"I think it's just fun and interesting, and also it gets the meeting off in the right mood," Hsieh says.

When Gordon Bethune was running Continental Airlines, he had a simple way for anybody in a meeting to jokingly say, "You lost me," or "I don't get it," or "That logic doesn't track for me."

They would simply call out the word *banana*.

He said the idea grew out of a bizarre experience he had with a former employer. People were kicking around ideas at a meeting and assumed they were following a line of reasoning to the clear and logical conclusion. But then the boss blurted out something nonsensical, leaving everyone puzzled. At a subsequent meeting with him, Bethune tried to anticipate where the discussion was headed, but he guessed wrong.

For Bethune, the experience—he said it was as odd as if someone suddenly said "banana" in the middle of a meeting—sent an unwelcome signal about his boss's management style.

"I knew then I couldn't work there anymore because I couldn't figure out the 'right' answer and because I couldn't think like he did," Bethune recalls. "I would never be successful in that environment as I didn't understand the rules of any logic he appreciated—there really weren't any."

But Bethune turned that experience to his advantage when he became CEO. In any group meeting, the logic can go off track, or people can't follow what somebody is saying. So Bethune told people in meetings that they could interrupt anytime and say "banana" if they felt lost. That way, nobody would take offense because they all knew it was rooted in a bizarre story.

"It was a funny way to talk about someone or something that didn't make sense," said Bethune.

Bringing a light touch to a meeting can be spontaneous, too. The trick is to make the best use of the context. Andrew Cosslett of InterContinental Hotels Group described how he turned what might have been a dreary setting for a meeting into an upbeat experience for his leadership group.

"When I brought this group of two hundred together, I was looking for a gimmick or something," he said. "And it just happened that we were meeting at a hotel in a room called the Courts of King Arthur Room. And it's got knights and suits of armor and old heraldic flags and oak walls, and that's where we happened to have chosen the conference to be. And I walked in and went, 'Oh, geez,' because it was dark. And then I thought, why don't I benefit from this—knights . . . knights. Oh, Knights of the Roundtable. That's what I could call this group. And I just sort of invented it on the spot. It came across like it had all been preplanned, of course, which is the serendipity of leadership sometimes. How you ad-lib is very important."

10.

SMART INTERVIEWING

You've no doubt heard the standard job-interview questions. What are your strengths and weaknesses? What do you see yourself doing in five years? What would your previous bosses say about you?

It's a familiar script, and most people are prepared for it when they come in for a job interview. (Everyone knows the storied response to the weakness question: "I'm so passionate and committed that sometimes I work too hard.") The ritualistic nature of the process makes it hard to figure out what the job candidate is really like, particularly when she sticks to her much-practiced remarks.

"After a while it's like Muzak," said Susan Lyne of Gilt Groupe, who has heard her share of canned speeches.

Out of necessity, CEOs have developed smart interviewing strategies to get people off their scripts, to get around the bullet points on a résumé. By the time candidates get to their office to interview for a job, they've likely been thoroughly vetted for their skills to ensure they have the technical capabilities to do the work. So it's up to the CEO to push, poke, probe, and prod for the intangible qualities about the person—the cultural "fit" part of the "fit and fitness" equation. The CEO is trying to understand whether this person can mesh with a company's culture well enough to make a contribution. He or she is trying to understand if the candidate has most of the five qualities discussed in the first section of this book, as well as other traits that are particularly important to that CEO. Hiring is also a gut call—kind of like dating—where small clues about a person's behavior and character can suggest good or bad chemistry. Just as in personal lives, CEOs bring their own values to the table, and they are looking for a good match that will complement the team.

"You know how it is when you meet people and you feel like you've known them for ten years?" said Omar Hamoui of AdMob. "That's not the case with most people, but it does happen with some people, and those are the kind of people I hire."

It is a tall order to be able to glean from an interview or two whether a person is right for the job and for the company, but with the right interviewing strategies, CEOs have found ways to quickly get an unfiltered sense of a person.

The Open-Ended Question

Most people walk into an interview expecting to talk about their experience and professional aspirations. Asking them surprising, open-ended questions will quickly get them off their scripts.

"I love asking people what the meaning of life is," said Michael Mathieu, the CEO of YuMe, an online video advertising firm. "I also say, 'On your deathbed, what do you want to be remembered for?' 'What's the most important thing that's happened to you over the last three years, something that's really changed your life?' I love asking those questions because the folks who are completely prepared are not prepared for those questions. I try to ask questions that give me a sense of the person's character and how they process information."

Linda Hudson of BAE Systems also uses an open-ended approach. "Okay, I've got your résumé," she will say to a candidate. "I've been over all the details. Just tell me about your life. Start wherever you want to, from the beginning or the end, but talk to me about you, what you've done, and then walk me through what you've done with your career.

"I find that the way people talk about what matters to them tells me an awful lot about how engaging they are, how committed they are, their energy level, their passion. And that's the sort of thing I'm looking for. I'm looking for the chemistry that would fit well in our environment and how articulate they are. Can they communicate effectively, which I think is extremely important. And it's more a subjective assessment. Do they have the people-skills part of what we need in the job? There are a lot of people who have the professional credentials, but do they have that extra something and the passion and people connection that sets them apart from others?"

Barbara Krumsiek of the Calvert Group said that one question she likes to ask is, "Wherever you worked before, what made it a good day?

"What I'm looking for is some reference to customers," she said. "I'm looking for executives or associates who understand that the customer is really the most important stakeholder in our world, and that they have to infuse every decision by thinking about the impact on the customer."

Family Matters

Several CEOs said they feel they can learn the most about people by asking questions about their families, friends, and social networks.

"I try to ask something that inspires them to talk a little bit about their family, whether it's their brother and sister, their parents, where they lived," said Meridee Moore of Watershed Asset Management. "I find that guys who have had strong relationships with women—whether it was their mother, their sisters, a teacher—tend to be secure in who they are, and tend to do well in our business. They have to work with me, for one thing. And they have to be able to challenge others and have me challenge them without taking it too personally.

"The other question I ask guys is if they've ever been in anyone's wedding party. If someone has asked him to stand next to him on the most important day of his life, at least one person thinks he is responsible. It means he's been able to establish and continue a relationship. It's not always true, but if you build strong relationships with people, you tend to go into a management meeting or a negotiation and come out of it with some respect. You go into it thinking, 'I'm going to leave this situation better than I found it. I don't have to kill everybody to get to the right result for myself.' These are good qualities in a person and a partner."

Tachi Yamada of the Bill and Melinda Gates Foundation's Global Health Program said he learns a lot about how someone thinks by hearing him talk about his family.

"It's usually quite an unstructured interview—where they come from, their family members," he said. "And then I try to understand how they deal with difficult interpersonal issues. Intelligence is often more displayed in what I would call complex abstract thinking, and there's nothing more complex and abstract than human relationships. And if they can work their way through a human relationship problem intelligently, my guess is that they're very smart people. Not that they can't add and subtract six-figure numbers multiplied by whatever, but that they can take a complex problem, break it down into its pieces, and figure out the best way forward."

Richard Anderson of Delta Air Lines said he can learn about the intangibles of a job candidate by hearing about her family and early life history.

"You have to probe a little bit deeper into the human intangibles, because we've all seen many instances where people had perfect résumés but weren't effective in an organization," he said. "So it's not just education and experience. It's education, experience, and the human factor—the situational awareness that a person has and that person's ability to fit into an organization and then be successful in the organization. It's a whole series of intangibles that are almost gut instincts about people. You want to know about their family. Where they grew up. What their parents did. Where they went to high school. What their avocations were. How many kids there were in their family. You know, what their whole background and history is.

"I learned that from a CEO I worked for. The CEO wouldn't really spend that much time on the résumé, but spent most of the time wanting to know everything about the person's life, family, what they liked, where they liked to go on vacation, what their kids were like. And it gave you a really good perspective about who they were as people. You spend more of your waking time with your colleagues at the office than you do with your family, and when you bring someone into that family—we have fifty senior leaders at our company and seventy thousand employees—you need to make sure that they're a fit to the culture. And that they're going to be part of that group of people in a healthy functioning way."

"What Makes You Howl?"

Some CEOs said their favorite question is simply: "What are you passionate about?"

They're not necessarily looking for jump-out-of-your-seat passion. They know quiet passion when they see it, and appreciate it just as much. They just want to know if the person they're interviewing is excited about something—whether it's work or something outside of work—because then they're a lot more likely to become passionate about the company they work for and the job at hand.

"I ask somebody to tell me what they've done that they are really proud of and tell me about it," said Steven Ballmer of Microsoft. "And if it's something you are proud of, you should be able to answer any question I can come up with, at least at a level that would satisfy my interest. I ought to be able to see your passion. It might be quiet passion; it might be bubbly passion. But I should be able to sense that you are one of those people who sort of throw themselves into things."

Jeffrey Swartz of Timberland uses some surprising strategies to find out if people are going to bring a level of passion and commitment to their work, or whether they just see the job as a way to earn a paycheck.

"If we're hiring a creative person from the outside, I like to call the headhunter a few days before and have them tell the person I'm interviewing, if it's an apparel person, to please wear their favorite pair of shoes to the interview," he said. "And if it's a footwear person, I ask them to wear their favorite outfit. And so the recruiters say, 'What do you mean by favorite outfit?' I say, 'I mean something that they can defend, as in, 'This is the most important piece of clothing that I own and here's why.' Or, 'These are my favorite shoes and here's why.'

"One guy came in wearing a navy blue Armani suit, a footwear guy, and I said, 'Wow. Is this the right outdoor thing?' And he said, 'I got married in this suit. This is my favorite piece of clothing on earth because it's like a wedding dress, but I get to wear it again and again. I don't wear it all the time because I'm not a suit guy, but you said to wear your favorite thing and explain it. It's because I got married in this suit.' I thought, 'I love this guy.' It's a way of asking what matters to you, and what doesn't.

"That's the other thing I like to ask people, and it depends who the person is, but usually I say, 'What makes you want to howl at the moon? What makes you really mad, so that you feel your pulse in your throat and you want to puke?' And the third thing that I like to say, especially to the creative crowd, because they travel a lot, is, 'When you're alone by yourself in a city, what do you do at night? And if I was going to hang out with you, what would we do together? What would you show me? What would you want me to see?' I don't undervalue the skills that people bring, but I don't need to vet that and I'm not even sure how good I would be at that. But Timberland is a place that demands my body and soul in some form or fashion, and so I've got to have some basic understanding of whether somebody is interested in that, or interested in that kind of a conversation."

Off the Charts?

Terry Lundgren of Macy's said he looks for a certain attitude because it's the one thing that people can fully control in their lives.

"Every morning you wake, you get out of bed, you decide, 'Hmm, let's see, on a one-to-ten scale, what do I want to be today?' You know, you have full control of that, and a lot of people don't realize they have full control of that. They think something's happened to them that's caused their attitude to go down or to go up, but we remind people that it's really theirs to decide every morning. And so I ask, 'Where is your attitude on a one-to-ten scale?' I want them to be honest with their answer, but it better be high. Because if they're honest and they say, 'You know, I really am about a four,' then I'll say, 'Well, sorry about that, and you need to go find some other people who will appreciate that. I don't.'

"My favorite answer is, 'I'm a fifteen.' Because I don't care that they go beyond the barrier I've set for them. I love people who say to themselves, 'I do wake up every morning, and I do choose to have a positive attitude, and I could be doing something else. I choose to do this because I love what I do, and I've got the right attitude to carry out my work in a positive way.'"

Mindy Grossman of HSN uses *Winnie-the-Pooh* as a reference point. She says she likes to hire people who are Tiggers, not Eeyores.

"They don't have to be loud, but I need energy-givers and I have to get a feeling that this person is going to be able to inspire people," Grossman said. "Are they going to be optimistic about where they're going? Are they going to attract people who are like that? I also need people who are able to stand up to me when they believe in something. I'm very passionate. I need people who are going to be able to make me look at things in a different way. So, I have to ask those questions, like, 'Give me an instance where you really believed in something and you were able to change the course and it was successful, whatever that was.' That's really important, because you don't want people telling you what you already know, or not telling you what you need to know."

Curiosity

Several CEOs said they ask candidates about the last few books they read. It's just one way of learning if the candidate is an eager learner.

"I think the one attribute that's really, really important to me is, are you curious?" said Sharon Napier of Partners + Napier. "And I try to ask that in all sorts of ways because if you don't really want to know how something works, if you don't read a lot, then you're not a very curious person. And in our business you really have to be. If I'm going to put you on an account like Kodak, I want you to learn how to make a photo book, and I want you to learn a little photography and I want you to learn how mothers keep memories. If you're not interested in digging in, then that'll say a lot about you."

Team Smarts

Many CEOs said they were looking for people who understood the value of teamwork and how to contribute to a team effort. They listen carefully to how often the person says "I" and "me" when they're describing accomplishments in previous jobs, rather than "us" and "we."

"I always find it helpful to ask who they do things with," said Tim Brown of IDEO. "How did this project happen? Who actually worked with you on it? And if they can very quickly give you lots of, 'I did this, and this person did that,' then you've got some hint about how collaborative they are. If, however, the answer is, 'I did this and I did that,' and 'I was responsible for that,' then you get no sense of who they work with and how they work with them. And then I worry that this is somebody who probably isn't very collaborative, probably isn't very good at promoting the ideas of others, probably isn't going to bring talent out very effectively. They may be a very inspirational person, they may do brilliant work. But they're probably not going to actually result in a more capable organization, which is what I'm looking for."

The CEOs also want to know whether people can lead a team, and make the people around them better.

John Chambers of Cisco said he likes to ask, "Who are the best people you recruited and developed and where are they today?"

To be an effective team player, and leader of teams, you have to be able to quickly assess people's strengths and weaknesses.

Vineet Nayar, the chief executive of the HCL Technologies consulting firm, asks a question of job candidates that undoubtedly takes them by surprise but gives Nayar a quick sense of whether the candidate can size people up quickly.

"I ask about the three or four people they interviewed with at HCL before they got to me," Nayar said. "I say, 'Today, you are their boss. Which one will you hire and why?' That's a question that has gotten me the right person all the time, because I know the three or four people you've interviewed with, and it gives me an idea how quickly you can find out their strengths and weaknesses. And then I ask the question, 'Would you hire me, and why? What did I say or ask that made a difference to you?'"

Jen-Hsun Huang of Nvidia said he uses a simple test to gauge whether a job candidate would be a collaborative colleague.

"I'll ask somebody to teach me something," he said. "They'll get on the whiteboard. I'll start saying things like, 'What if you did that?' People who are really receptive to brainstorming and creativity will say, 'Huh, that's interesting. Well, what if we did that?' Somebody who doesn't like criticism will say, 'That's been tried. It doesn't work.' So those people tend not to be good collaborators."

Challenges

Most people have faced difficult challenges and failures in their work. CEOs assume that. What they want to hear is how you dealt with them, to get an insight into how you handle adversity.

"One of the first questions I ask is, 'Can you describe a decision you made, or a situation you were involved in, that was a failure?'" said Susan Docherty of General Motors. "And I don't need to know how they got to the failure. But I need to know what they did about it. How they handled that is the best illustration of whether or not they're innovative thinkers and are comfortable taking some risk."

When industries are shifting so quickly, you need people who can persevere to make things happen—the qualities of fearlessness, and an ability to handle adversity and failure. Many CEOs said they ask about failures and the toughest challenges people have faced.

"I try to get them to talk generally about some of their toughest challenges," said James Rogers of Duke Energy. "I ask them to talk about their failures, how they dealt with it, how it made them feel, the point when they knew they were failing. I ask them to talk about things they've taken on that they weren't so sure of, but went at it step by step. The way they describe how they embrace a new idea, or how they've redirected their career in some way, gives me a sense of who they are."

Ambiguity presents its own challenges. Clarence Otis of Darden Restaurants said he tries to find out if the person he's interviewing can handle working without a clear road map.

"Being comfortable with ambiguity and uncertainty is a trait I look for, because those folks are pretty comfortable with diversity, and not knowing how people who have differences might react in a situation doesn't unmoor them," Otis said. "They're comfortable with it and may even like that. Those kinds of folks also, when they're faced with ambiguity and uncertainty, have got their wits about them, so they're looking as much for the opportunity that's inherent in that as they are for the risk. You ask them about the various experiences they have had, and you try to probe. 'Where were those circumstances where there wasn't good direction, when it wasn't clear how things would break?' How do they respond to those questions? What's the narrative around how they thought and behaved in those environments?"

Self-Awareness

When you're part of a team, do you understand the role you play, based on the kind of person you are? Do you know what you're good at, and what you need to work on to get better?

Tony Hsieh of Zappos has a clever way of digging into this issue. "One of the questions I like asking the most is, 'If you had to name something, what would you say is the biggest misperception that people have of you?' Then the follow-up question I usually ask is, 'What's the difference between misperception and perception?'"

Hsieh explained what he was trying to understand about a person by asking those questions.

"I think it's a combination of how self-aware people are, and how honest they are," he said. "I think if someone is self-aware, then they can always continue to grow. If they're not self-aware, I think it's harder for them to evolve or adapt beyond who they already are."

Niki Leondakis, the chief operating officer of Kimpton Hotels and Restaurants, said she wants to know what skills people are trying to develop more, as a way to gauge their self-awareness.

"If someone can't answer that honestly and rather quickly, if you have to think too hard about what you're working on developing, are you really working on it?" she said. "I'm looking for a commitment to self-development and personal growth."

Some CEOs ask candidates how colleagues might describe them.

"One of my favorite interview questions is, 'If I had four of your direct reports sitting in a room, how would they describe you?'" said Nancy McKinstry of Wolters Kluwer. "Just the adjectives they pick are always pretty instructive. Then I turn it around and say, 'If I had four of your last bosses in the room, how would they describe you?' Everybody obviously is always going to put the best light on it, that's the nature of an interview. But you do get a sense of the individual in that process, and that kind of becomes instructive about how they think, how they operate in a team environment, how they would fit in with the culture of the company."

"Why Are You Here?"

Do you want to work at this company, or do you just want a job?

This is a key question that CEOs want answered. They want to know if people have done their homework, and believe in what the company does and its mission.

Some leaders are blunt. Bobbi Brown, the founder of her cosmetics company, said she simply asks people, "Why do you want to work here and what do you love?" Judith Jamison, the artistic director of Alvin Ailey American Dance Theater, gets right to the point as well. "When they come to my office, I say, 'Hi, how are you? What do you want this job for? Why are you here? Do you know how hard this is?'"

Shantanu Narayen, the CEO of Adobe Systems, uses a little more indirection.

"My first question is always, 'Tell me what you think this job is all about,'" he said. "And I've found that allowing them to speak about what they want to do, and what they think the job is about, is actually very, very useful, because it illuminates what they think they want to do in the company. I typically also end an interview with asking them how they can make a difference. I don't think there is a right answer, but I think you know by the response to the first question, which is, 'What do you think this job is about?' When candidates speak more to what they want to accomplish and how they think they can make a difference, and why Adobe is a great place, or why that would be challenging and exciting, those are clearly, quote-unquote, right answers, because they're talking about how they can make a difference. If they talk about specifics as it relates to title and people, I would say those are headed in the wrong direction."

Anne Mulcahy, the former Xerox CEO, said the answers to questions about why a candidate wants to work at Xerox are probably the best indicators of whether somebody is likely to succeed at her company.

"I want to know why they're choosing us," she said. "Not so much why we should choose them but why would they choose Xerox. I want to hear the rationale as to what they're thinking about in terms of what they could do for the company and why they think it would be a place they could be successful. Have they done their homework? Do they understand the place? Do they aspire to the kind of value system and culture that we have here? Is there some passion for why they're on the other side of the desk wanting to be a part of our organization?"

Susan Docherty of General Motors has a good approach for

finding out not just if people have done their homework about the company, but also if they have a sense of the challenges facing Docherty herself.

"I always ask people, 'If you could be in my shoes today, what would be the top three things you'd do?'" she said. "When most people prepare for an interview, they're very focused on their prior experiences and examples of what they've done. And I think that you really do get some very candid, on-the-spot thinking when you ask them what they would do if they had my job. It demonstrates to me how they think on their feet without being prepared. Sometimes I get answers back that are very in-the-moment, tactical answers. Sometimes I get very leader-like questions about vision, about things that are way beyond stuff that we're currently thinking about. I love that question, because it's very telling about how people think. And then there are other people who give a very balanced view, with thoughts on the short-, medium-, and long-term. So I get a real quick read on strategic versus tactical thinking. And it's nice to get an outside perspective of how these people view me as a leader and hear what they think I should be focusing on, versus what I really am focusing on. I love that question."

It helps for job candidates to be able to articulate the reason, concisely, why they want the job they're applying for. Jilly Stephens of City Harvest is listening to hear if a candidate can explain that in a couple of sentences. Not many can.

"What is it that appeals to them about the job they're interviewing for? That's always quite an interesting opening question, and I'm always surprised at the number of people who can still be answering it fifteen minutes later," she said. "I'm looking for people who are passionate about whatever job it is that they're applying for here at City Harvest, and that they're passionate about our mission: to help feed hungry New Yorkers."

A Writing Sample

Some CEOs know that a piece of writing can provide a window on the way job candidates think. "Sometimes you can tell somebody's intelligence just by reading what they've written," said Cristóbal Conde of SunGard.

So they demand to see a piece of writing. They are sometimes surprised by what they see, and this test can change their mind about someone, to the upside or downside.

"It's the best way of finding out all sorts of things," says Nell Minow of The Corporate Library. "Do they have a sense of curiosity about the world? Are they just repeating things they've read, or is there some sense of engagement with it? And their ability to express themselves, I think, is tremendously important—their vocabulary, their sense of appropriateness of communication. Ultimately I won't hire anybody who can't write. I ask for a writing sample, the best example of their writing. And they'll say, 'Well, do you want a paper I wrote in school, or do you want a memo?' I tell them to give me what they think is the best example of their ability to communicate. I'll read it for their precision, their vocabulary, their sense of appropriateness of communication. If they're using texting language in a memo, that's a bad sign."

The Shared Meal

Many CEOs said an absolute must of the hiring process is to share a meal with someone, because it's a good way—outside the controlled environment of an office—to find out what somebody's really like. It can be small things. Are they indecisive about what to order? Do they talk down to the busboy? Can they read social cues and keep a conversation going?

"It's like a microcosm of life," says Carol Smith of the Elle Group.

But those small things can quickly add up to a deal-breaker, and many candidates have lost job opportunities based on their performance at a restaurant.

"I never hire anyone without having a meal with them," said Teresa Taylor of Qwest Communications. "I am absolutely convinced that that's how you see what people are really like. You can tell by the way they order, you can tell by the way they treat the waitstaff, you can tell by the way they drink too much or what they drink—you can pick up all these lifestyle things that you can't get out of questioning them sitting in your office. Maybe they can't make a decision on what to order, or they're very snotty to the waitress. I absolutely have changed my mind on individuals after seeing that."

Niki Leondakis of Kimpton Hotels and Restaurants said that she uses a meal at a restaurant to watch carefully how a job candidate treats the service staff.

"I think people get a little more comfortable, and I can observe how they walk through a restaurant and whether they barrel through or let other people go first," she said. "Or when we're sitting down and the server comes to take the order, do they respond by looking him in the eye, or do they talk to waiters without looking at them, as if they're invisible? It's very telling to me how someone treats the service staff."

Similarly, candidates should be careful about how they treat people at the company before they meet the CEO.

"I'm going to see how they treat the receptionist," said Jana Eggers, the CEO of Spreadshirt, a company that sells personalized clothing online. "I always get feedback from receptionists. I'll want to know if someone comes in and wasn't polite, didn't say hello, or ask them how they are. It's really important to me."

The Danger of Rushing

As much as these questions can improve the chances of hiring well, nobody has a perfect record in picking candidates. When asked what, in hindsight, were the reasons why a person didn't work out, CEOs often said they were overly impressed by their résumé, or they were in a rush to hire.

"Typically there was some external pressure to fill a job," said Barbara Krumsiek of Calvert Group. "And really, I have to remind myself that there's no pressure so great to fill a job. None. I don't care how long it takes. Because the mistakes were made from hiring too quickly. They're not bad people. They just weren't right in our setting. I'll take a year to fill a key position. I'd rather live without someone than suffer the consequences. And it is very painful to hire incorrectly."

11.

LOCK YOURSELF OUT
OF YOUR OFFICE

The corner office is just one of the rewards for the hard work and sacrifice required to earn the top spot in a department, a division, or a company. But the physical office itself? It can be a trap.

That may be an exaggeration, but not by much. Many CEOs offer the same advice: To keep tabs on what employees are thinking and saying, executives have to make the time to get out and walk around, and they have to find other ways to learn what people are really thinking. The less time spent in the office, the better, even though it's easy to feel as if they're more productive there. By walking around, they will find out what people are thinking about the company and their leadership. Managers have to be adept at making employees feel comfortable so that they share their thoughts openly. Yes, it can be time-consuming, but by all accounts, CEOs say that the investment of time delivers enormous rewards on all fronts—employee retention, insights on company strategy, and worthwhile feedback.

The corner office is also isolating, CEOs say. Information is massaged for the boss. People generally want to bring only good news. Many CEOs have developed strategies to get a sense of what people think of the company and the leadership. These include walking around, reconfiguring offices to create a more open layout, developing relationships (including through e-mail) with trusted sources throughout the company they can rely on for unvarnished opinions, and by asking employees for direct feedback.

The point is to do something to counteract the phenomenon that Nell Minow of The Corporate Library said was crystallized in a piece of advice she received from her business partner, Bob Monks, when she moved into a corner office: "Watch how funny your jokes become." Anyone who's ever sat in a meeting where the room erupts after the boss tells a so-so joke knows how true that saying is. But it also serves as a metaphor for, as Minow explains it, "the challenge that gets tougher and tougher as you get higher in the organization to get people to be honest with you."

Get Out There

Deborah Dunsire of Millennium said that management-by-walking-around is essential—not just for getting feedback, but also for retaining talented employees.

"I schedule walk-around time so that I can be in different buildings just stopping by offices," she said. "Typically people used to jump. Now they don't do that anymore. I would just say, 'Hey, what's keeping you up nights? What are you working on? What's most exciting for you right now? Where do you see we could improve?' That's really rewarding. What I do find is that it's easy to get into an ivory tower mentality if you don't do it. So, in other words, all the information the CEO is getting is being processed and managed. And if you never have direct access, or you don't create forums to hear what people are really thinking, then you can have a divergence between what you believe is the case within the organization and what actually is.

"I think that's where organizations lose momentum, lose engagement, and start losing great people. One of my core beliefs is that the work of leadership is about ensuring that we have the right people within our organization. You do that through actively knowing the people, knowing what they value and believe, how they believe the company can improve and taking action on it. To me, that walking-around time is feeding that business objective. So it then becomes much easier to afford the time because it's driving a critical business objective."

Cristóbal Conde of SunGard uses visits to clients with his salespeople to get unfiltered feedback on the company.

"I do my best to see a client every day, and I go there with a rep or the account manager," he said. "Let's say we're in the subway or a taxi or whatever and we're heading to the client. The rep is getting ready for this meeting and kind of going through everything. What the rep is not ready for is all my questions. Their guard is not up when I ask about the organization. 'What's your number-one issue? If there's one thing you could change, what would it be? If you couldn't be at SunGard, what would you do?' Very quickly you get insights. And I'm not saying that you then act on them, but you kind of build a giant mosaic about what your organization really looks like, and people respect that."

Bill Carter, a partner and co-founder of Fuse, a youth marketing agency, said he learned an important lesson about how he spends his time in the office when he returns from road trips.

"One of the things I do more of now, and probably a better job of now than I did ten years ago, is being really present in our office when I'm there," he said. "I think many senior people—CEOs and presidents of companies, both small and large—obviously spend a lot of time outside of the office. What I used to tend to do with the 50 percent of the time that I was in the office would be to go into my office and shut the door, literally or figuratively, and delve back into the real core responsibilities of that day or that week.

"I might as well have not been in the office. I wasn't interacting with other staff, both senior and junior staff. I wasn't gauging anything that was going on with the staff, learning anything new, or understanding the challenges that people were facing. I've learned that when you're in your office and you're in that position, the best thing you can do is spend at least 50 percent of your time in the office communicating with as many staff as you have time to communicate with. Holing yourself up in your office is not the way to learn about what's happening in the organization. The information doesn't flow up to you when you're in a closed-door situation like that.

"I think that if you look at your core responsibilities a little less literally, you'd probably want to spend more time with your staff, because what are most CEOs really in charge of? Well, they are in charge of setting strategy. They are in charge of creating the best work environment. They are in charge of finding the best talent. How can you possibly do that by isolating yourself in your office and only communicating with people from accounting or your outside legal counsel or the majority of the people that are probably the ones e-mailing you? Your junior staff people are not e-mailing you. And if you don't go down the hall and talk to that person, you're not going to know the real challenges."

Terry Lundgren of Macy's likes to make unannounced visits at stores around the country. Though there's always an initial surprise when he shows up, he said the experiences are always valuable.

"I've always really worked hard at communicating in both directions—listening and having open dialogue with lots of levels of the organization and doing it formally and informally," Lundgren said. "I've been doing this for many years, and I'm sort of known for this; I just go and pop into a store. I have the cell-phone number of the store manager, and I call him from the cosmetics department, and 95 percent of the time he's there. The managers have a small heart attack at first and sometimes they say, 'This isn't Terry Lundgren, come on, who is this?' And I say, 'No, it really is. Just come on down to the floor, and I'll say hello.' I literally do it every week somewhere. And so we walk through the floor, and they have had no time to prepare for my questions, they've had no time to prepare the store, and ultimately, they view it as a good experience. I always make it a good experience.

"If I have my issues or concerns or my complaints, I generally don't take it out on that store manager. I would take it back to management about what we're doing at the store to not make it as good a shopping experience as it needs to be. I learn as much by going through a store as I do from anything I do, much more than sitting in my office at my computer or holding a big meeting here in New York, because I'm learning and seeing exactly what our customer is seeing, and there's no preparation for me. As much time as I spend in the stores—and I probably spend more time than most CEOs in the stores—I want to spend more time in the stores because I never come back saying, 'Boy, that wasn't a good use of my time. I need to spend more time in my office.'"

Brian Dunn, the CEO of Best Buy, also visits stores, and he approaches his company like a customer so he understands the experience.

"I think the CEO job is designed to insulate people from things that really happen," he said. "I want to make sure that I'm sort of out there in the white noise and the messiness of it all. If you don't, you run the risk of becoming insulated and ineffective. One of the things that became pretty clear to me, in my last role as president and chief operating officer at Best Buy, is that people don't line up outside my door to tell me how they've screwed something up. You know, you sort of get the 'Yep, everything's going terrific and it's A-okay.' So it's really important to me to get out where the customer experiences the brand, and that means I surf our Web pages. It means I call our call center. It means I visit our stores and talk to our associates about what's working, what's not."

John Donahoe of eBay will often reach down a few rungs in the organization to ask people for their input. He also finds that people on their way out of the company are a reliable source of insights about how the company is operating.

"I try to talk to different people at different levels," Donahoe said. "It's interesting how much companies don't like that. The people I contact like it, but their bosses or their bosses' bosses don't. One of the things I've also found really useful over time is that any time a senior person leaves, or sometimes a mid-level person, I'll often reach out and say, 'Hey, would you either send me an e-mail, or I'd love to get together and I'd love to hear what the three things are that you think I should know about what's going on in the organization that you think I might not be aware of.' And then, secondly, 'If you were me, what would you do differently from what we're doing?' And I find that when people are leaving, they're often in a very reflective state. And because they've often made a very difficult decision, they're also stunningly direct, because it's like they have nothing to lose. In fact, if they care about the company they'll be more direct. And I find I get some very good insights because they're not sugarcoated. They're direct, and they're often quite actionable."

Trusted Sources

Remember Nell Minow's expression about how funny your jokes become once you're a manager? Every boss needs people in the organization who are going to tell her that her jokes aren't funny—in other words, give her straight feedback, because they aren't cowed by titles or rank. Often personal assistants play that role, or vice chairmen. But it's necessary to keep cultivating such relationships—in person or through e-mail—for a simple reason: the more feedback, the better.

Ursula Burns of Xerox noticed an immediate change when she moved from the president's job to the corner office.

"One of the things that happens is you become a little bit more isolated," Burns said. "You've got to work at it every day. There are people you've been friends with, or have a different relationship with, that you have to make sure you keep. There's one—a superstar guy on our staff—and I'm able to talk to him, and he's able to talk to me at a different level, almost like a non-boss. And so he's the guy who can be really clear and say, 'You're just absolutely wrong,' or 'I don't agree.' I also have people on my staff with completely different styles. It's really important to have those different perspectives. My CFO has absolutely no qualms about saying what he thinks, period. 'That's it. You can like or not like it. This is what I think.' And that's good. I happen to have a team of people who actually give me the closest thing to unfiltered feedback that you can get."

Gary McCullough of Career Education Corporation said he has found that e-mail, in addition to management-by-walking-around, is often a useful tool for gathering insights.

"When you're at the corporate headquarters, what you're getting is not always the truth because it's been filtered a number of ways," he said. "So I walk around and I ask questions. I think the best way to do it, to figure out what's really going on, is to travel to the other company locations, and to have town-hall-style meetings. I tend to have pretty open Q&A sessions where I tell the truth, as much as I know. I also send out, on at least a quarterly basis and sometimes more frequently, all-employee e-mails. I help them understand what our results were, what some of the issues are, what some of our priorities should be. And since I've been doing that, I've gotten responses back, sometimes from only fifty employees, sometimes from as many as two hundred or three hundred employees. And I do my best over the course of a couple of days to respond to every one of those e-mails. So I've actually got people in the organization that I've established dialogues with over the course of the last couple of years who will send me notes that say, 'Have you thought about this?' Or, 'You should know this is going on in our company or in our location.' And I treat every one of those pieces of information with a great deal of respect. I protect their anonymity, but it gives me a good picture of some things that are going on that I otherwise wouldn't know.

"I'll ask some questions. They will give me insights. They'll give me suggestions. Sometimes they'll be pretty tough on me and I've always said, 'Thank you for the feedback.' I've never once gone back on somebody or got anybody in trouble. And so the more I've done it, I think the more they say, 'I sent the guy an e-mail. He responded and he wasn't even mad.' I'm glad that they have enough faith and trust that I will protect them, if they say something that I need to know, or that they feel that I'm open enough to take their feedback. Many times, all I do is write, 'Thanks for sharing the information.' And that's good, too."

Redesign the Office

One way to avoid the isolating trap of the corner office is to eliminate the corner office—either by creating an open-plan layout, or making other adjustments, to encourage more open communication.

Joseph Plumeri said that when he arrived at Willis Group Holdings in 2000, he discovered that the chairman had his own floor and his own elevator. To send a signal that things would be changing at Willis, he took drastic action. He removed the doors from everybody's office, including his own. (If anybody at Willis needs privacy, they can go to one of the conference rooms, which do have doors.)

"They thought I was nuts," he recalled. "But I wanted to stimulate conversation."

Meridee Moore of Watershed Asset Management had worked once in an office herself, and didn't like the experience. When she moved to Lehman Brothers, she was in a more open-floor plan. "I loved it," she said. "Everybody worked together in a sort of mosh pit of ideas. It was more fun, more energizing, and I realized that you do better work if you get input from people around you."

That experience influenced her decisions about how to design Watershed's offices when she started the company.

"We sit in one big open room," she said. "It's the ultimate flat organization. We all have the same size desks. I can hear how the analysts are communicating and asking questions. There are no interoffice memos or office hierarchies. There's not much that is distilled or screened. When we're working on something, there's a lot of back and forth."

Omar Hamoui of AdMob went one step further. His company has an open-floor layout, but he doesn't stay in one place. He moves his desk around a lot to stay in touch with what people are thinking at his fast-growing company.

"About every six weeks or so I move to another part of the company that I feel I haven't heard a lot about lately or where I don't know the people that well, and I sit there," he said. "My whole desk construct is nomadic. I just pick up my computer and sit somewhere else. If people see you sitting there and you're not doing anything, they walk up to you and talk to you. It's pretty effective in terms of hearing how things are going and how people are feeling about the company or how people are feeling about you. If you make yourself available to people, they'll tell you what they think. I hear a lot both from my direct reports as well as from people generally at AdMob about how things are going. That has to do with making sure that people are comfortable talking."

Susan Lyne of Gilt Groupe also works in an open-office layout, and she said she'll never go back to a traditional office.

"It's transformational on many levels," she said. "People stop by my station without an appointment to get a question answered or run an idea by me. They're still respectful if I'm clearly working on something, but I'd much rather risk the occasional interruption than go back to the isolation I often felt in a big corner office. I no longer need an HR report to get a handle on the mood of the company. There are messaging benefits as well. Being on the floor signals that I consider myself part of—not above—the team. And at a company that is growing as fast as Gilt, it allows me to meet new employees much faster."

To make sure people don't hold back on sharing insights, Lyne adopted a strategy she first heard about from a Google executive, Marissa Mayer: office hours.

"I try to do it two hours a week, when anyone from our company can book half an hour with me," she said. "It's turned out to be a fantastic way to find out what's bubbling under the surface. A surprising number of people will book time with me who are significantly down the food chain. And in some cases it's because they want to have a little face time with me so that they can get noticed. But there's always something that's on their mind. And when you are running a company it's very hard to get below a certain level, maybe one level below your direct reports. It has multiple benefits. It gives me a way to get to know people a little better that I pass in the hallway or I see in the Monday all-hands meeting. But it's a great early warning system for something that may be either misunderstood or a challenge within a department. It's hugely valuable."

Just Ask for Feedback

Want to know what people think of the job you're doing? Sometimes, all you have to do is ask for feedback—a particularly efficient way of getting a sense of what people are thinking away from the corner office.

"I ask simple questions like 'How am I doing?' 'What should I do differently?' said Carol Bartz of Yahoo. "At first, people are shocked when you ask them that. They won't answer right away because they actually don't think you're genuine about it, so you have to kind of keep probing and make it safe. They eventually will come around and tell you what they're thinking."

Kevin Sharer of Amgen used a more structured approach to solicit feedback when he became CEO.

"It was announced in December of 1999 that I was going to take over as CEO in May 2000," he said. "I'd already been the president of the company for six or seven years. So I was well known, but I hadn't supervised R&D, and that's obviously the heart of Amgen. So I posed several questions to the senior staff: What are the three things you'd like to make sure we keep? What three things would you like to change? What is it that you would like me to do? What is it you're afraid I'm going to do? And then, finally: Is there anything else you want to talk about?

"I talked to the top 150 people in the company one at a time for an hour. I invited them to bring in, if they wished, written responses so I could have them. I took very careful notes. I wasn't trying to sell anything. I was trying to deeply listen. And in a science-based company, we value data, and this was social data of profound importance. So I synthesized all the answers and I wrote, just before I became CEO, here's what you guys told me and here's what I think about it, and so here's our priorities. People were enthusiastic and honest in talking to me, and it also helped me to get to know the top people in the company better."

The approach, Sharer said, stemmed from the idea that he considers himself a coachable person. Like many CEOs, he regularly gets input through "360 reviews," and learns from it.

"I'm sincerely open to and I seek feedback, because that's the only way that you can grow as a CEO, which is a very isolating job," Sharer said. "And so if you don't create mechanisms to get authentic feedback, you won't. Every year I have the head of human resources at Amgen who reports to me conduct an evaluation of me done by my team that they write up and then present to me and the board. And that's an uncomfortable process, of course. You hope, as CEO, for the team to say, 'Boy, boss, you did a great job this year, are we lucky to have you.' And by gosh, every year they've come up with three or four things that are quite authentic that I ought to do better. So you've got to create those kinds of feedback loops.

"I've been given feedback that says, 'Kevin, sometimes you come to a conclusion or blurt out something in a meeting that is premature, which tends to stifle debate, and you know something?—you're wrong.' And so I'm very mindful of letting the conversation proceed and trying to be more Socratic in the way I lead rather than dictatorial and impulsive. So that's one place. Another one is, sometimes I will go too deep—what they call my submarine mode—too early in an attempt to try to understand the issue. So I try to moderate that and let issues come to ripeness in terms of when we're ready to actually make the call. So a lot of this is not undergoing a personality change, because that's not possible. It's just being aware of what your tendencies are. If you think about it in terms of golf, I'm standing on the tee, the water's over there to the right, and my tendency is that I'm going to yank it right in the water. So I'd better know that and try to counteract that tendency. So it's a lot about self-awareness."

Dan Rosensweig of Chegg often uses annual performance reviews to ask for feedback on how he is managing.

"I ask employees, 'If you had my job, other than giving yourself more vacation and a raise, what's the first thing that you would do that you don't think we're doing yet?' I try to make the review process more comfortable by asking people: What do you need more of from me? What do you need less of from me? What is it that I'm doing that you would like me to stop doing completely? And what is it that I'm not doing enough of that you'd like some more of?"

12.

BE A COACH, NOT A CRITIC

Many bosses are from the school of management where they focus solely on results. Did you do a good job? Did you do a bad job? In this sense, it's an approach not unlike that of a critic. Thumbs up, thumbs down, how many stars do you get for the latest work you've done? Then on to the next task.

It's certainly an easier approach to management, because it involves sitting back, watching the work, and rendering judgment. If people doing the work aren't good enough, they can be replaced. Smart workers often get better in spite of bosses like this, just by studying the feedback loop and learning from it, or by seeking help from their colleagues. Then the boss pats himself on the back, saying, "I'm a good manager," even though he has spent little to no time actually managing or leading anything.

Sound familiar?

Here's another approach: Be a coach, not a critic.

As a coach, a manager's job is to elevate individual players, make the team better, and try to give guidance and input on the front end rather than just take potshots on the back end. His job is to give feedback in a way that's not personal, so that employees know he has their best interests at heart and that he's on their side. While many managers try to avoid what might be difficult conversations about an employee's performance, a coach considers it his responsibility to have such talks. Employees know if their boss is rooting for them to succeed, and they're much more open to feedback if they sense that their manager's goal is to make them better. If you assume that most people want to get better, that they want feedback and advice, that they want somebody to care about their future, then giving feedback becomes much easier. Isn't that the x-factor that makes the difference between somebody being a boss and a mentor? When somebody talks about a great mentor she's had, she generally means that the person was a teacher, an adviser, someone who helped prepare her for future challenges by passing along insights and advice. Sure, the relationship between a manager and an employee is more complicated, but a boss will get more out of the people who work for her if her goal is to make them better.

Deborah Dunsire of Millennium said that giving feedback was part of caring about an employee.

"I learned it's important to be forthrightly honest and candid in feedback," she said. "Even if it's negative, it's really helpful to people, particularly people who really want to improve. What helps you do that—and not kill their motivation—is deeply caring about their advancement and growth. So if you deeply care about their advancement and growth and you constructively but candidly tell them what they need to do to improve, it's like gold. I think the challenge is always how the message is delivered."

Tachi Yamada of the Bill and Melinda Gates Foundation's Global Health Program learned an important lesson from a former mentor about giving feedback, and it shaped his thinking about his responsibilities to coach and elevate people rather than focus on their shortcomings.

"Morton Grossman was one of the founders of modern gastroenterology," Yamada said. "I remember he once gave me a paper to review. I was young at the time. He said, 'I want you to review this paper.' So I spent a couple of evenings reading the paper and wrote a six-page review of it. I shredded the analysis. And I showed it to him, to show how smart I was. He looked at it and said, 'Okay, now I want you to write me a report and give me a reason why it's a fantastic paper and how we could make it even better.' And I did. And from that viewpoint, actually, the paper wasn't bad.

"This applies to people, too. It always comes down to people. One of the things I've learned is that you can't go into an organization, fire everybody, and bring in everybody you want. You have to work with the people you have. I've gone into different organizations in completely different walks of life several times, and you walk into the organization and you realize that some people are very good, some people are average, and some people are not so good. And if I spend my time focusing on everything that's bad, I'll get nothing done. Or I could say, what are really the best things about the people I have? What makes them great, and how can I really improve them one or two notches? And if I spend my time on that, then I'll have a great organization. Everybody has their good points. Everybody has their bad points. If you can bring out the best in everybody, then you can have a great organization. If you bring out the worst in everybody, you're going to have a bad organization. So that lesson, while it was about reviewing papers, has been a critical element of my management style."

For Will Wright, the video-game developer, having a deep understanding of the people who work for him is essential to making them open to feedback. Like many other CEOs, he also assumes that people are eager to be coached on how to improve.

"A lot of the people I've managed—artists, programmers, producers—they don't just want to know if they are doing a good job or not," Wright said. "They want to be pushed and challenged in their careers. So, if they feel like you are presenting things to them in such a way that a year later they are definitely going to be better artists or better programmers, then it really feels like a win-win. Even if you give them tough critical feedback, they see the benefit and value of it, as opposed to just a typical performance review.

"For a lot of people, their jobs and their positions are not the relevant part of how they see themselves. They have an internal view of themselves, their career aspirations, the direction they want to go. The really important motivational stuff is more in their secret identity. A lot of that has to do with talking to them. You want to spend a fair amount of time exploring their interests, what they do outside of work. Usually people have some passion that drives them. And this to me is one of the important points of working collaboratively with other people—trying to get a sense of what the one thing is that makes their eyes light up, that they get excited about and won't stop talking about. And if you can get a sense of what that is from somebody, and you can harness that, that's going to have more impact on how they perform their job, how they relate to you, how you can convey a vision to them in a way that they get excited about it. For me that's the real key to a lot of this stuff—exploring and understanding the personal passions that people working with you have."

∾

Too many companies use annual performance reviews as the only opportunity to provide feedback. But such reviews have limited usefulness because they put off for up to a year conversations that should be happening in real time. By then, the reviews may carry too much weight, and employees—starved for feedback—read too much into them, or focus on what is not said, or fixate on a phrase and take offense. Or the reviews give a once-over-lightly treatment to end the year on a positive note.

Some CEOs said they would like to do away with performance reviews altogether. Carol Bartz of Yahoo said she prefers the "puppy theory" of providing immediate feedback.

"When the puppy pees on the carpet, you say something right then because you don't say six months later, 'Remember that day, January twelfth, when you peed on the carpet?' That doesn't make any sense. 'This is what's on my mind. This is quick feedback.' And then I'm on to the next thing. If I had my way I wouldn't do annual reviews if I felt that everybody would be more honest about positive and negative feedback along the way. I think the annual review process is so antiquated. I almost would rather ask each employee to tell us if they've had a meaningful conversation with their manager this quarter. Yes or no. And if they say no, they ought to have one. I don't even need to know what it is. But if you viewed it as meaningful, then that's all that counts."

Lawrence Kellner of Continental Airlines said his experience of feeling blindsided by puzzling feedback from a former boss influenced his thinking about how he coaches employees.

"One of my first bosses was nice and friendly during the whole job, didn't say a word," he said. "And then I got this performance review at the end with comments that would have been nice to know during the process. One, I didn't agree with him, but two, it didn't matter. He was the boss and I fully respected that, but it's kind of hard for me to read his mind. He made me look like I did a terrible job, and yet I walked into the room thinking that this would be pretty good feedback. And so I learned an important lesson about communicating up front, right away, and I think that was probably reinforced by my best bosses. They gave me lots of feedback as I was going along, so even if things didn't work out perfectly, it sure wasn't a surprise when we talked about where we were."

His approach now?

"Short, clear, and direct," he said. "My general view is the first time I tell you something—I mean it may just be my view of the world—that's not a bad one on you. If I keep telling you the same thing and you keep doing the other thing, that's when we have a much tougher discussion."

There is no single right way to give feedback, and managers may want to try different approaches to see what works best for them. Even on the simple matter of how to handle conversations to give feedback, leaders use a range of strategies.

One is the "criticism sandwich" used by Dany Levy of Daily-Candy.com.

"I joke sometimes that everything I needed to know about management I learned from working with emotionally disturbed kids, which I did for two summers," she said. "I don't mean this in a negative or derogatory way. But there are some basic principle human skills that I learned about this, like the criticism sandwich—praise, constructive criticism, praise."

David Novak of Yum Brands prefers to give praise first, then feedback, and he carefully avoids use of the word *but* between the two.

"The best way to give feedback is to start out with, 'This is what I appreciate about you.' They might have great strategy, good vision, they're good at execution, or whatever you think they're really doing well," Novak said. "When you start out by talking to people about what they're doing well, that makes them very receptive for feedback because at least you're giving them credit for what they've done. Then I say, 'And you can be even more effective if you do this.' I think that really works."

The reason he avoids *but*?

"I think 'but' can be a killer word," he said. "'And' really recognizes the appreciation part. If you say 'but,' it throws all the appreciation stuff out the window."

Tachi Yamada prefers not to mix positive and negative feedback.

"One of the things I've learned is that it doesn't matter how many good things you say, the one bad thing is what sticks," he said. "So therefore feedback should be viewed in the context of time, not in any one specific episode. If I have something negative to say, I will say it. I will be clear about it. But I won't try to couch it in a lot of positives, because people have a natural tendency to not want to hear a negative message. So I try to do it as quickly as I can, and I try to do it in the moment. But I also try to give positive feedback in other moments. To try to mix the two is often very hard, because the positive messages get lost in the one negative message, and the negative message gets garbled."

Niki Leondakis of Kimpton Hotels and Restaurants said she has learned to hear a person out before giving feedback, which makes the person more open to being coached.

"One of the things that has evolved is learning to listen first when there's a problem or a situation that needs to be addressed," she said. "Rather than sitting down with someone and telling them what's wrong or what needs to be addressed or what needs to be fixed, I ask how this came about and what's happening here, and listen to the back story. How'd we get here? Why does this look like this? And then, when I have understanding about it, I can then turn it into a coaching moment rather than a moment of judgment and fear and intimidation for the person on the other side of the table who's listening to what's wrong with their performance.

"When I was a younger manager, my anxiety about what wasn't right drove me to confront things quickly. The faster I confronted it, the more quickly it could get fixed. It would get changed, and while that's a good thing, the manner in which I did it frequently left people feeling defensive. So by listening first and trying to understand how we got here and their story, I think it allows them to then hear my point of view. And then we can move into solutions. When people feel judged right out of the gate, it's hard for them to open up and listen and improve."

This listen-first approach helped Lisa Price, the founder of Carol's Daughter, the beauty products company, overcome her unease in giving feedback. Looking back, she said she took such discussions far too personally when she first starting working as a manager in the television industry.

"I was a head writer's assistant in television production, so the other writer's assistants reported to me," she said. "And it's not something that I was very good at, because I like to be people's friend. It's not that I need everybody to like me, but I'm a very autonomous person when I work. So when someone says, 'This is what I need you to do,' I focus on it, and I do it, and I don't have to be micromanaged. I don't get distracted. So I tend to think everybody else is like that. And when I would come back to someone, figuring that they were done and they were only a third of the way through some work, I'd say, 'What's going on? What happened? Why aren't you finished?' I had to learn that everybody wasn't like me. It was good training for what I do now.

"I just had to accept that I was the one who was the most uncomfortable. It took a little while for me to realize that. I was thinking that the other person is more like me, and I'm going to come and tell them that they're not working efficiently, and they're going to be offended. I did it a few times, and I saw that the person appreciated the feedback, or they would say to me, 'Well, I was having a hard time because I didn't understand what this meant over here.' And then it becomes more collaborative, and you're listening to their perspective, and we figure out a way to make it work. And the person who's most uncomfortable is really me. So if I can deal with being uncomfortable, then I can get past this. I had built it up in my head to be much bigger than it actually was."

Cristóbal Conde of SunGard developed a simple system for providing feedback that ensures that nobody feels singled out in his company. It's a system he developed over time, and after he learned some difficult lessons about the hazards of micromanaging.

"Early on, I was very command-and-control, very top-down," he said. "I felt I was smart, and that my decisions would be better. I was young, and I was willing to work twenty hours a day. But guess what? It doesn't scale. Now, there are plenty of incredibly successful companies run by micromanagers, and that's a different story. The last year I did that, I was away from home 302 nights, not including day trips. I had to fly around all over the place making all the decisions. And I would walk in, make an uninformed decision, get on the next plane, go somewhere else, and repeat the process. I look back at that year; I don't think I got anything done.

"That was in the early nineties, and that experience convinced me that the right way to do it is to do the opposite, which is to hold people accountable, to really restrict the number of things you say to them, and to decide on the one or two things that are the most important. And then when you meet with them, you always bring back the conversation to that one thing. You have to do that consistently for over a year before you start having an impact."

Conde has also changed the way his company does performance reviews to reflect a consistent approach.

"A boss once told me, 'Cris, you're a smart guy, but that doesn't mean that people can absorb a list of eighteen things to do. Focus on a handful of things.' Very constructive criticism, and the way I've translated that is, when I do reviews, everything is threes," Conde explained. "So, 'Look, Charlie, these are the three things that are going well. These are the three things that are not going well.' Now, that's very important because then people know that everybody's going to get three positives and three things they should do differently. Then they don't take it personally. I've found that to be an incredibly valuable tool."

A coaching approach can be used in bigger meetings, not just in one-on-one conversations. It's an attitude that can be reflected in any context—how to make things better rather than simply judge what was done in the past.

"I hate Monday-morning quarterbacks," said David Novak of Yum Brands. "So I try to focus my meetings on building and sharing know-how that will help us win going forward. I focus my meetings on beating last year. Why is this program that you're talking about going to be better than what we did last year? What do we have in the pipeline that's going to keep us successful?' With every meeting I try to focus on what's the 'so what' of what you just told me. And then, what's the 'now what'? What are we going to do now so that we can get better results? I like to learn from what happened, but I want the focus of my meetings to be forward-looking."

Many CEOs have learned important leadership lessons playing sports. While sports metaphors are common in business, they are nevertheless useful in the context of learning how to give feedback. In sports, this is what coaches do—giving constant feedback in practice to help people get better and help the team win.

Bill Carter of Fuse said that his leadership philosophy was influenced by his years playing lacrosse in high school and college.

"I grew up in Maryland in an area where lacrosse was the dominant sport," he said. "And I happened to go to a high school that was the dominant program in the country, and it was run by a coach named Joe McFadden. I don't remember losing more than three games in all of high school. I was in this culture of winning, where all the coaches, the players, the kids in that high school, and the administrators expected us to win.

"I was recruited to play lacrosse in college by a mediocre team at the time—Gettysburg College in Pennsylvania. And again, by sheer luck, the day before I was to go on campus as a freshman, I received a letter in the mail that the lacrosse coach had retired, and a new coach was coming, named Hank Janczyk. Again, there was this culture of winning, this expectation that every practice was going to be unbelievably competitive. Every game was judged not only on whether we won or lost and what the score was, but on how we played. He's still there twenty-something years later. And today, he's one of the top lacrosse coaches of all time.

"I think that experience has definitely carried over for me, not only the expectation of winning and creating a business culture about winning, but also about whether it was the best that we were capable of doing, not just based on the outcome. I think about that a lot in the context of our business now, about when we go into a new business pitch. If we win, I still evaluate the pitch and whether it was the best portrayal of who we are, or whether we won for some other reason. And I think about that at times when we lose new business pitches or don't do an exceptionally good job for a client in the client's eyes. I can still look at that and evaluate it based on factors other than the final result."

Carter said his approach to managing at work is to be fair, honest, and direct in a helpful way.

"If you want people to be at their best, and if you want the whole company to be on the same page all the time, you need to be willing to communicate directly with people," he said. "In our office, what we've achieved is that being direct is not a personal attack. I did learn that, to some degree, in my college lacrosse experience. When my coach was coming down on me or somebody else, it never felt like a direct attack. Now, it did feel awful, but I never thought he was being mean-spirited about it. I never thought he was doing it for any other reason than he wanted us, as a team, to be on the same page and to be the best that we could be."

PART THREE

LEADING

13.

CREATING A SENSE OF MISSION

What's the difference between management and leadership?

Management is about results. You're given certain assets—people, money, equipment—and you're expected to make the most of them to deliver an expected outcome. Management is quantifiable, measurable, almost a science. Companies can gain a significant edge by being adept practitioners of the discipline.

Leadership is an art. It's the secret ingredient that makes workers commit more of themselves to their work, to make the extra effort, to make the work personal and not just a job, so that they identify themselves with it rather than just shrugging and saying, "Hey, I've got to put food on the table, right?"

People report to managers, but they follow leaders.

In the previous section of this book, CEOs shared their insights on how to be effective managers by making the most of their time, running useful meetings, and hiring good people through smart interviewing techniques. They also shared their experiences and ideas on how to give and get feedback.

In this section, CEOs talk about leadership and the different strategies they use to get employees to fully identify themselves with the job and to feel invested in their work so that they see it as part of their lives. There's an expression: "Some work to live, and others live to work." When people are committed to what they do, the line between work and life dissolves.

Leaders who can create a sense of mission are far more likely to succeed than their competitors, because they will have harnessed that extra energy.

It's easier for some organizations to create a sense of mission than others. Certainly for many nonprofits, it is a clear goal that attracts many people to the organization in the first place.

"One thing that I really try to do is to spend a lot of time focusing on why we're here," said Tachi Yamada of the Bill and Melinda Gates Foundation's Global Health Program. "The mantra has to be about nine million babies dying, and to get people to have a visceral sense of what that is—a city the size of New York filled with babies disappearing every year. The magnitude of it is hard to comprehend. And so I try to work with a sense of urgency and try to instill that urgency in the people around me."

At Teach for America, Wendy Kopp noted that the goal of trying to improve the quality of education in inner-city schools draws many applicants. "Maybe this is easier in our endeavor than some," she said. "We're looking for people who are magnetized to this notion, this vision, that one day all children in our nation should have the opportunity to attain an excellent education. And that magnetizes certain people. And so it's more about them—it's their vision, it's not my vision. It's our collective vision."

Add in the profit motive, and the task can get a bit trickier. After all, at a certain level, the reason companies exist is to deliver profits to their owners—the shareholders in the case of a public company or, if it's a private firm, the founder, partners, or investors.

But if you assume that employees like to be a part of something bigger than themselves, and to work toward an ambitious goal—whatever it may be—then the job of leaders is to set a goal that people can believe in, beyond the price of a share of company stock.

"We preach a lot here that team is one of the most beautiful of all human experiences," said Kip Tindell of The Container Store. "You do great things together, and you go home at night feeling wonderful about what great things you accomplished that day. That's what people want, and that's what wise and sophisticated leaders help cultivate and know that people want. Every bad boss you or I have ever had thinks that what people want is the exact opposite of that."

There is no formula for creating a sense of mission, though certainly one necessary ingredient is conviction, since nobody will follow a leader who doesn't believe wholeheartedly in what he or she is saying.

Lofty Goals

Apple is often talked of as a place where people want to build products that will change the world. IBM has an effective marketing campaign about building a "smarter planet." At Zynga, the mission is "Connecting the world through games." These are what Jim Collins and Jerry I. Porras, the authors of the book *Built to Last*, dubbed "BHAGs" (the acronym, pronounced Bee-hags, for Big, Hairy, Audacious Goals).

Andrew Cosslett of InterContinental Hotels Group set an ambitious goal for the company when he took over.

"When I first arrived I did a video, and I said we're going to be one of the very best companies in the world," Cosslett said. "Not the very best hotel company—we're going to become one of the very best companies in the world, and here's a few things that that means to me, but we'll have to work out together exactly what it takes. That's gained a currency in the business now because it's aspirational. It's something people find compelling. And because most people actually do want to improve and move on and succeed and be on a winning team, they say they like that."

Guy Kawasaki of Alltop and Garage Technology Ventures is an entrepreneur, but he is also a former Apple executive and the author of many books, including *Selling the Dream*, about evangelizing products, based in part on his own experiences at Apple.

"I learned from Steve Jobs that people can change the world," Kawasaki said. "Maybe we didn't get 95 percent market share, but we did make the world a better place. I learned from Steve that some things need to be believed to be seen. These are powerful lessons—very different from saying we just want to eke out an existence and keep our heads down."

Kawasaki shared some of his insights on how to create a sense of mission.

"The foundation is the desire to make meaning in the world—to make the world a better place," he said. "We believed in the Mac division that we were making the world a better place by making people more creative and productive. Google, at its core, probably believes it's making the world a better place by democratizing information. So it starts from this core of how you make meaning, which translates into some kind of physical product or service that actually delivers. How are you making people more creative, more productive? How are you disseminating information? How are you giving people peace of mind?"

You don't have to run a company like Apple or Google to create a sense of mission, Kawasaki said. Every entrepreneur can do it.

"It's kind of all how you look at it, right?" he said. "We'll take an extreme example. Let's say you are a street-food vendor. You can look at it like you go to Price Club and you buy hot dogs cheap and you buy buns cheap and then you grill them and you sell them and you make your buck or two or whatever you do on each of them. Or you can look at it like you're part of the fabric of downtown San Francisco, you're part of the charm, part of the ambiance of a tourist area. It's kind of pushing the limits of romanticism, but at some level it's all mental. It's a matter of perspective."

Alan Mulally of the Ford Motor Company also talked about the importance of perspective in creating a sense of mission at his previous company, Boeing, and now at Ford.

"I think the most important thing is coming to a shared view about what we're trying to accomplish—whether you're a nonprofit or a for-profit organization," Mulally said. "What are we? What is our real purpose? And then, how do you include everybody so you know where you are on that plan, so you can work on areas that need special attention. And then everybody gets a chance to participate and feel the accomplishment of participating and contributing.

"I've been very fortunate to be part of projects that are really big and broad. Airplanes are some of the most sophisticated designs in the world, four million parts flying in formation, and it involves hundreds of thousands of people all around the world. And the same is true now at Ford, with our full product line.

"So they're very big, large, compelling visions, and the biggest thing I've found is that the more everybody comes together on the real purpose, the higher order of that, the better. Is the airplane really about an airplane or is it about getting people together around the world so they can find out how more alike they are than different? And is a car about just a driving experience or is it about safe and efficient transportation, and your family, and freedom? And so the higher the calling, the higher the compelling vision you can articulate, then the more it pulls everybody in."

To illustrate the point further, Mulally offered a variation of Peter Drucker's famous story about stonecutters.

"One of my favorite stories is an analogy where this reporter stops by a construction site and he interviews three bricklayers. He asks the first bricklayer, 'What are you doing?' And he says, 'Well, I'm making a living laying these bricks.' The reporter says, 'Oh, that's great. That's very noble.'

"He asks the next bricklayer, 'What are you doing?' And he says, 'Well, I am practicing the profession of bricklaying. I'm going to be the best bricklayer ever.' And the reporter asks the third bricklayer, 'What are you doing?' And he says, 'I'm building a cathedral.'

"There is technical excellence and professionalism, but we all want to contribute to making a cathedral," Mulally said. "And the more we feel that and know what our part in it is, the more I think you can take the team performance to a whole other level of excellence."

Competition

People love to compete, of course, so another way to marshal the collective energy of a workforce is to establish a clear scoreboard to measure performance against competitors, and then reward the team when it wins.

Gordon Bethune, the former Continental Airlines CEO, used that strategy to rally workers to help turn around the long-troubled carrier. He wanted Continental to have a standout reputation for providing clean, reliable, safe transportation. Bethune told all the employees that their main gauges of success were going to be how they performed against the other airlines on key service measures. And if they beat them, he said, the company would save money, and some of it would be shared with workers.

"I own a twelve-hundred-acre ranch, and it's got a seventy-acre lake," said Bethune, explaining his philosophy of getting employees motivated behind a common goal. "It's wonderful. And do you know, in spite of all that, I still have to use bait when I fish? Can you believe it? The point is there's got to be something in it for the fish, and it's up to me to know what the fish like. It's not up to them. So maybe if I learn enough about the fish and what they like, they might be easier to get in the boat and provide me a little recreation.

"So when you look at forty thousand people saying, 'We want to be successful,' well, how do you measure that? How do you measure success? And what do they win if you win? And what is the outcome then? Why do they care if the CEO is successful or the company's successful? So you have to define success. Clearly it means there's got to be measurable goals that everybody understands, and then you start strategizing on how to get there, and figure out how everybody wins. So at Continental, we said, 'Okay, we're going to win, and we'll define winning as not just staying alive, but beating our competitors.'

"Success was defined by customers, as getting them to their destination safely, on time, with their underwear. Pretty simple measures. When you start getting people to their destination safely, on time, with their underwear, reliably day after day after day, you start pulling the better customers away from your competitors. They recognize that there's value there. So next thing you know, we're getting a pay raise because we've made some money. We're on time. We've got an on-time bonus. And we have profit sharing for employees— 15 percent of pretax income got distributed to employees. All of a sudden we say, wait a minute, winning is defined by the investors as making money. Winning is defined by customers as getting there on time. We all win together, or nobody wins. It works in all team sports. So all the infighting starts going away. All the competing for scarce budget resources goes away."

Creating a sense of teamwork can be done in more subtle ways, too.

Drew Faust of Harvard University said she got some good advice about how to create a sense of mission at the university that transcended the goals of the individual schools on campus. The insight came from Michael E. Porter, the Harvard Business School professor.

"I asked him to run a session at the first deans' retreat of my presidency," she said. "I said to him that one of my goals was to build more cohesiveness and integration across Harvard to make it really one university, and to help these deans help me invest in that notion. So we talked about what he might do at that meeting to enhance my goal and enable me to move the deans, as a group, toward that.

"So one of the questions he asked that deans' group is one that I've returned to again and again. He said to the deans of the individual schools, 'How does being part of Harvard University give you an unfair advantage?' What he meant by that is, if you're Harvard Law School or Harvard Medical School, how are you able to be a better medical school or better law school—in other words, to do your job as a dean better, to meet your own aspirations as dean of your school better—because you're part of this larger organization.

"And it was just the right question for what I wanted to accomplish, because it allocated to the deans both a self-interest in buying into the larger university purposes but also the aspiration of thinking about how we all can be better together, through making schools more integrated, making the university a part of how we think about how the individual schools operate."

Communication Is Leadership

Once you've established what your organization's mission is, you must repeat it endlessly. CEOs said they've learned that doing so is necessary to make their message stick, even if they feel as if they've said it many times before. Not everyone will hear it the first time, and even if they hear it, they may not hear it the same way.

Here's Drew Faust again:

"One lesson I've learned has to do with communication. Someone would say, 'Well, you've never talked about X,' and I'd say, 'I've talked about that here, here, here. I talk about that all the time.' Then I realize that 'all the time' isn't enough. You have to do 'all the time,' and more. As a scholar, you don't want to repeat yourself ever. You're supposed to say it once, publish it, and then it's published and you don't say it again. If someone comes and gives a scholarly paper about something they've already published, that's just terrible. As a university president, you have to say the same thing over and over and over. That's very important."

Susan Docherty of General Motors made a similar point:

"Whether you have a really small team or a really big team, communication needs to be at the forefront. It needs to be simple. It needs to be consistent. And even when you're tired of what the message is, you need to do it again and again and again. Because everybody listens at different levels, and everybody comes to the table with a different perspective and a different experience. And the same words mean different things to different people. On some very key things, people need to internalize it, and they need to own it. And when they do, you'll know that you're effective as a leader, because you hear them saying it."

Many CEOs agree on this point—that there is a need for relentless communication. Without it, employees have a way of filling in the blanks themselves and making incorrect assumptions.

At The Container Store, the executives take this philosophy one step further. One of their core principles is that communication is not merely a tool for leadership but leadership itself; the act of sharing information helps to create a sense of mission.

"We believe in just relentlessly trying to communicate everything to every single employee at all times, and we're very open," said Kip Tindell. "We share everything. We believe in complete transparency. There's never a reason, we believe, to keep the information from an employee, except for individual salaries. I always make it a point to give the same presentation I give at the board meeting to the staff, and then that trickles down to everybody in the company. I know that occasionally some of that information falls into the wrong hands, but that's a small price to pay for having employees who know they know just about everything."

Voters and Volunteers

The fundamental relationship between employers and employees has been redefined in recent decades, particularly at large companies.

These firms used to win the loyalty of workers by being paternalistic organizations that offered rewards for sticking around. So it was a lot easier to believe in the organization if it was truly going to take care of you, as General Motors was once able to do, back in the day when its lavish health care and retirement benefits earned it the nickname Generous Motors.

Implied contracts for lifetime employment are very rare now, of course. People are far more willing to move around. They don't expect to work their entire careers at a single corporation. They see themselves more as free agents willing to go where they can be recognized and appreciated, and where they can grow and learn. So some CEOs believe they can win loyalty not only through a paycheck, but also by treating employees like voters or volunteers.

"We talk a lot about execution and the importance of it," said Anne Mulcahy, the former Xerox CEO. "But I actually think it's a lot more about followership—that your employees are volunteers and they can choose to wait things out if they don't believe. And that can be very damaging in a big company. So it is absolutely this essence of creating followership that becomes the most important thing that you can do as a leader."

How to do that?

"It's fundamental communications, in terms of your ability to get out there and be with your people, tell a story," she said. "People really have to begin to believe in a story to get passionate about the direction the company is going in, which hopefully you've been able to do through the way you articulate it, simplifying the complex so that people can get their arms around it and see how they can make a difference. There's nothing quite as powerful as people feeling they can have impact and make a difference. When you've got that going for you, I think it's a very powerful way to implement change."

Daniel Amos of Aflac said he thinks of leadership more like politics, in that employees need to be won over like voters to get their support.

"In business, you should treat your employees like they can vote," he said. "It doesn't mean you're going to get everybody to vote for you. But you kind of try to kiss the babies and shake the hands and tell them you appreciate them and would like them to support you. You can do it like a dictator, but I'm not sure very many of them in the long run are successful. I think that if you can create the vision and get them to follow it, you're a lot more successful than if you demand they follow it. So, I tend to run it more like politics than the Pied Piper of leading."

Symbols Say It

Some companies print laminated wallet-sized cards with the company's core values on them. The point is to give people constant reminders of the mission, what the company stands for. Some people may be tempted to dismiss such cards as silly, but many CEOs said they found symbols helpful in driving home their message.

Joseph Plumeri of Willis Group Holdings talked about how he used a small idea—by his own admission it was a bit corny—to pull people together when he took over the company.

"I had no experience outside the United States when I got to Willis," he said. "Willis is the oldest insurance broker in the world and had never been run by anybody but a British citizen. And so

Joe Plumeri shows up. Not only am I not British, I am as un-British as you can be—an Italian kid from New Jersey they actually called Fonzie who came to run the company. So I had to get these people excited. People talked more about yesterday than tomorrow, more about memories than dreams. And you try to reverse all that stuff. So I was in a diner in Plainfield, New Jersey, one night, and I drew a flag and put 'Willis' on it.

"A little thing, just to try to get them to think in terms of this one flag, and everybody would wear a lapel pin to show they're all part of this service. So if I have a client in New Jersey, but they need help in Italy, then because of that one-flag service, they're going to help them over there rather than be part of their own fiefdom. I find that in big companies, you often have silos and fiefdoms, so you've got to break them down. If you don't break them down, then you've got a confederation of just countries and people, and you're never going to be great.

"So I handed out these lapel pins. In America, everybody wears a lapel pin. But in many other countries, nobody wears these. They think I'm nuts. But in thinking I'm nuts, it tended to be unifying. I had everybody in a big meeting in London, and I said there's 'One Flag,' and 'One Flag' was the approach. I said I want global service—with resources delivered locally so everybody can do their own thing and have the global resources at the same time. And so I made a big deal out of the pins. There was a big buzz in the room about the pins. So the talk of London is this silly Italian American with these pins. And then the company started to do better. We went public. The company did well. And then they were wearing the pins not as a joke, but to say, 'I work at Willis.'

"You've got to try to do things. I really do believe that as hokey as that stuff sounds, you're dealing with people. I don't care whether they've got ten degrees or no degrees at all, they want to get excited. It was corny, but I've always felt a sense that doing things to get people's attention is good, because human beings for the most part like stuff like that. I think they'd rather be in a company that's kind of exciting than one that's not. And so if you try to do something spectacular, or something that motivates them, and if it falls on its face, it was a good shot. You give it a shot."

14.

SMALL GESTURES, BIG PAYOFFS

My first job with the *New York Times* was as a freelancer in the Detroit bureau in 1991, covering the auto industry. I had given up a better-paying job—and benefits—as the business editor of a medium-sized newspaper near New York to move our young family to Detroit for a chance to work at the *Times*. After several months, I got a call from a competing newspaper. I was twenty-nine, married, and we had a one-year-old daughter, so I was naturally looking for a full-time job. I interviewed with the other newspaper, and they offered me a job. But my goal was to work as a staffer for the *Times*, and the *Times* countered with an offer to bring me back to New York as an entry-level reporter. I was thrilled.

But one of the most vivid memories from that time was a note I received from John M. Lee, an assistant managing editor at the *Times*. He had dashed off a quick, handwritten note after the *Times* agreed to hire me for a staff position.

"Hurry back," it said. "We need you."

It probably took him all of a minute or less, but that note remained tacked to the wall at my desk in the final weeks before I left Detroit, and I made sure to bring it with me to New York. It was a stressful time in our lives—in the space of about eight months, my wife had lost her teaching job in New York because of state budget cuts, we had moved ourselves in a U-Haul out to Detroit, our daughter had developed what seemed to be worrisome health issues (they later turned out to be nothing), and we moved back to New York.

In those storm-tossed days, John's words—"Hurry back. We need you"—felt like an anchor.

I was reminded of the note from John, who died in 2009, many times as executives shared stories of the power of a small gesture, or a brief investment of time, that paid off with endless dividends. People remember such gestures years later, and they engender a strong sense of loyalty and commitment. (Over the years, I've seen many notes tacked to cubicles with comments scribbled from various bosses about a job well done.) I know I would have run a marathon's worth of extra steps for John Lee if he had asked.

~

If business is like politics, then discussions about a company's mission are like stump speeches—words to whip up the crowd and get them to say, "Yes, I believe in you, you have my vote."

But there is a reason why politicians "walk the rope line" and go door-to-door to shake hands: to connect at a personal level. It may not be particularly efficient, but they do it because they know the gestures are important and they know that these voters will then become ambassadors for the candidate, and advocate for him or her with their friends and relatives.

With all the pressing demands on managers, it can be easy to focus only on the biggest priorities or plow through endless e-mails. But many CEOs said they made time for the small gestures—the handwritten note, the phone call, taking time to drop by an office to chat—because they recognize their power.

If business is measured by return on investment, few things can match the effectiveness of small gestures. The payoff can be enormous.

When he was running Continental Airlines, Gordon Bethune said he always made time to swing by break rooms in airports to talk with his staff.

"I tended to get overscheduled, but if I had a flight at two o'clock, I would probably never get to the airport later than twelve-thirty," he said. "I'd spend an hour just going down to the crew room, or walking around. That's how I met a lot of people. That's how I was very visible. When you actually take the time to go over to somebody's office and personally thank them, whether their office is in a cockpit of an airplane or in a break room downstairs, that's an actual manifestation of interest in them. You actually care enough to go say thank you. If you're interested but don't show it, it's the same as disinterest. And you need to take the time to show the people who work for you that you're interested in them, and that includes the second-shift baggage handler. So I would schedule my time like that.

"But you know, the best compliment I ever heard came one Christmas Day. I always went out to the airport on holidays. I always made sure that I was there and I'd thank people for giving up their holiday to work, and we'd go down to the break room. I'd always eat in the break room where the free food was being passed out. And I went to sit down at this big long table with these two guys, and I said, 'Anybody sitting here?' One guy said to the other one, 'I told you he'd be here. Give me my ten bucks.' He had bet that guy ten dollars that I'd show up.

"So how much does it cost to run down to the break room and say hello on your way to wherever? Not that much. What's the potential? Unlimited. So your accountant can't get that correlation, but if you know what you're doing, you know that you've got to make that investment. Your job for the shareholders is to get the most money you can get in the marketplace. To do that you've got to make some investment, and a whole lot of it is you personally. You work it every day. If you're not willing to pay that price, you'll probably be mediocre, and your competitors will probably beat you."

Gary McCullough of Career Education Corporation shared a story about a small gesture from his days in the military and how it influenced his leadership style.

"I'll never forget one of the interactions we had with my commanding general of the division in which I was a platoon leader," he said. "We were at Fort Bragg, North Carolina. We had miserable weather. It was February and not as warm as you would think it would be in North Carolina. It had been raining for about a week, and the commanding general came around to review some of the platoons in the field. He went to one of my vehicle drivers and asked him what he thought of the exercise we were on. To which the young private said, 'Sir, it stinks.' I saw my short career flash before my eyes at that point.

"He asked why, and the private said, 'There are people who think this is great weather for doing infantry operations. I personally think seventy-five and partly cloudy is better.' And so the commanding general said, 'What can I do to make it better for you?' And the private said, 'Sir, I sure could use a Snickers bar.' So a couple days later we were still moving through some really lousy weather, and a box showed up for the private. And that box was filled with thirty-eight Snickers bars, which was the number of people in my platoon. And there was a handwritten note from the commanding general of our division that said, 'I can't do anything about the weather, but I hope this makes your day a bit brighter, and please share these with your buddies.' And on that day, at that time, we would've followed that general anywhere. It was a very small thing, and he didn't need to do it, but it impressed upon me that small gestures are hugely important.

"It's the private things that go a long way, as well. In my current job, there's a woman who is a couple of levels down from me, and I found out that her father had died. I sent her a quick note just to say, 'I'm sorry to hear this. If there is anything that I or we can do for you, let me know.' But to this day—two years later—she still reflects back on that. Again, she's several levels down in the organization, but she has been overtly supportive of the work that we've done in the organization. And I think I won a fan that day, not because that was my goal, but because it was the right thing to do for her."

Recognition for a job well done can also have an outsized impact. Joseph Plumeri of Willis Group Holdings said he devotes a lot of time to making sure staff members are recognized for their efforts.

"I've always felt that in people businesses, there's never a limit to how well you could do as long as you're able to continue to motivate people to do better and better," Plumeri said. "Machines are built to go so far, and then you've got to get rid of the machine and get a new one. But with people, you can constantly make them better if you work on it, and you can get them excited and create the right environment. What I learned is that a sense of recognition—patting somebody on the back—is as effective in Japan as it is in Germany, as it is in Texas. Nobody has ever said to me stop with the congratulations. Stop with the enthusiasm. It's a universal language. I think it's a big deal. I go and take pictures with everybody and send them a copy of the picture, and send little notes. It's a big company, but we do a lot of that stuff because I really believe that little things like that are just ways that people get motivated. And people like me should never forget that people get excited over being recognized for what they do, and it's not all about money.

"A lot of people ask me, 'How do you spend your time?' And I tell them I spend 25 percent or 30 percent of my time calling my own associates. I have a system of people feeding me information about our employees and I call them, whether they have a family problem, or somebody has died, or whether they have pulled off a great deal and brought in a new client, or saved a client. It's a two-minute, three-minute phone call, or a handwritten note. I can't begin to tell you how important that stuff is, and I believe in it."

A simple "thank you" can also go a long way, said Dan Rosensweig of Chegg.

"We spend a lot of time in all of the companies that I run or work in making sure we know who the star performers are, rather than forcing them to send an e-mail or come see you or brag about themselves, which they are really uncomfortable doing," he said. "I call them and say, 'How are you? I understand that you are a star performer. You are knocking the cover off the ball. I just want to say thank you and let you know you have an open dialogue if there is other stuff that you think we need to be doing.' So I do a lot more of that because I know I would appreciate it. I've learned that they appreciate it because they then can focus on doing the job and not worry about whether people are noticing."

David Novak of Yum Brands shared a story about floppy chickens, and the importance of recognition.

"Our culture is based on the notion that there's an innate need for well-deserved recognition, and it's universal," Novak said. "Using recognition is the best way to build a high-energy, fun culture and reinforce the behaviors that drive results. I think what makes our culture unique is that we have a tremendous amount of fun and positive energy coming from recognizing others. I'll tell you how I got to that. When I was running operations for Pepsi, I'd always go out in the field and I would do these roundtables with the route salesmen at six o'clock in the morning. I was in St. Louis and I was asking everybody about merchandising. Who's doing great merchandising? What's it like with our customers these days? And then everybody'd start talking about this guy named Bob. And Bob was at the end of the table and they were saying, 'Well, Bob's taught me more about merchandising than anybody else in our company. I learned more from him in three hours than I did in my first four years here when I went out with him in his route truck.' And they were raving about Bob. Well, Bob is down at the end of the table there and he starts crying. And I said, 'Bob, why are you crying?' And he said, 'Because I've been in this company forty-two years. I'm retiring next week and I didn't know anybody felt this way about me.' This was the first time he heard people raving about how great he was.

"So I said to myself, if I'm going to be in a position where I can make a difference and lead an organization, I'm going to make recognition the biggest value I have in our company. Because the worst thing is for people to work hard and not feel appreciated for it. When I became president of KFC, I wanted to break through the clutter on recognition. So I gave away these rubber chickens that we called floppy chickens. I'd go into a restaurant and I would see a cook who'd been there for twenty-five years and the product was great. So I'd give him a floppy chicken. I'd write on it, and take a picture of him with me, tell him his picture was going to be in my office and I would send him a copy of the picture. And then I'd give him a hundred dollars because you couldn't eat a floppy chicken. This was unbelievable. The whole place went nuts because it was so different. There had never been a president who had that much fun with recognition and I found that people really loved it.

"After that I was the president of Pizza Hut, and then, when we were spun off from PepsiCo, I became the head of this company and I made recognition a major value of ours. And I found out that recognition works everywhere. Every leader in our company is expected to have their own individual recognition award. The Taco Bell president has the sauce packet award. The president of Pizza Hut gives away cheese heads. This works everywhere. I went to China and I gave a Yum Award to this restaurant manager. When somebody on our operations team went over to China, she asked that same manager if she could see his Yum Award. And he said, 'No.' And she said, 'What do you mean, no?' And he said, 'It's at home locked up in my father's safe.'

"All the walls in my office are covered with pictures of people I've recognized all around the world, with floppy chickens, cheese heads when I was president of Pizza Hut, now all my Yum awards. And people say, 'What happens when your walls fill up?' I said, 'I'm going to put the pictures on my ceiling.' When people come in from all around the world, they all want to see my office. It symbolizes what's most important in our business, which is people."

Novak then explained how he makes sure the right people are recognized.

"I think there are two things that are very important about recognition," he said. "One, it needs to be deserved. And two, it needs to come from the heart. So I think what leaders have to do is recognize the people who are getting it done. For them, it can't be done too much. Why be selfish on the thing that matters most to people? People leave companies for two reasons. One, they don't feel appreciated. And two, they don't get along with their boss. We try to recognize the people who are really getting it done anytime they happen to get it done. If you've got to err on the side of anything, recognize more than you should. I call it the privilege of being a leader. The privilege of leadership is being able to recognize the people who are getting it done for you."

Small gestures can also help defuse uncomfortable situations. Terry Lundgren of Macy's described how a quick detour on the way to a difficult meeting helped set a more constructive tone.

"When we announced that we were buying the May Company, I went out and visited all of their regional divisions," he said. "I remember going to one of the first ones, and it was an obvious place that we were going to eliminate because we had a big Macy's headquarters in San Francisco, and they were in L.A. We would have one office for California, and they were very nervous. And so I went with a couple of my senior people, and we were going to have this fancy lunch at a Hilton Hotel. And we were driving there from the airport, and we went by an In-N-Out Burger, and I said, 'Stop, turn around. Let's get a Double-Double for everybody, and some might want two." A Double-Double is the single best hamburger in America. So I brought thirty Double-Doubles and great french fries to this meeting. I just walked in and I said, 'You know, I just figured you guys are going to be a little uptight about this meeting, and I just got to California. I haven't had a Double-Double in six months. I want to have one, and I thought I'd be rude if I had one and I didn't offer one to all of you guys.' And people started clapping. They were from Southern California, so they knew about In-N-Out Burgers, and it just kind of broke through. And we all sat around and ate these hamburgers while we were having an open conversation and dialogue. And it turned out to be one of the best meetings we had. They were feeling that this was going to be a real tense situation, and so I think breaking those barriers down is really important."

15.

TYPE A TO B

To reach the corner office, it takes a lot of ambition, impatience, and a fierce determination. To stand out from the pack, you have to do more work than others—and do it better and faster. It certainly helps to have a few of the classic traits of a Type A personality.

But once they've won the top job, many CEOs said they've had to learn how to pull back and listen more so that they are not dominating every conversation and meeting. It is one of the trickiest balancing acts for a CEO. While his job is to create a sense of urgency in his organization to stay ahead of competitors, he must also slow down—and act more like a Type B personality—to get the most out of the people around him. He has to signal to his subordinates that their input matters (even if the CEO feels he knows the answer already), to let them stub their toes occasionally so they can learn the lessons themselves, to quiet his own go-get-'em personality so that others can emerge as leaders, and to dial back so he does not overwhelm and micromanage his employees.

For first-time managers and CEOs alike, the lesson is the same—you have to rein in many of the skills and instincts that got you there, and ask in each new situation, "What am I here for? What can I do to contribute the most right now, to elevate the result?"

Several executives told revealing and instructive stories about their struggles to make this transition. In many cases, the lesson did not come easily or early since it required them to step away from what they had always done best—the actual work—to let others do it.

Steven Ballmer of Microsoft, whose energy and outsized personality is the stuff of legend in corporate America, said one of his goals as a leader was to learn to slow down.

"I race too much," he said. "My brain races too much, so even if I've listened to everything somebody said, unless you show that you've digested it, people don't think they are being well heard. Sometimes you really don't hear because you're racing. It's just the way my brain works. My brain is just chop, chop, chop, chop, chop. And so, if you really want to get the best out of people, you have to really hear them, and they have to feel like they've been really heard. So I've got to learn to slow down and improve in that dimension, both to make me better and to make the people around me better."

Like Ballmer, Joseph Plumeri of Willis Group Holdings comes across as a big personality. He explained how he learned that leading people was not about trying to continually inspire them and pump them up.

"I grew up with role models—including my father—who were very strong individuals," Plumeri said. "That was a good thing, because when you grow up with the tutelage of strong people who have strong opinions, it makes you strong. And then you add your own personality, which in my case is big dreams, anything's possible, zeal and dreaming and hard work, and believing that if you work twenty-four hours a day you can accomplish anything. But you get to a point where you realize not everybody wants to work seven days a week, and not everybody has this as their main passion in life. I think passion's important. I talk about that a lot. And you find that you can wear people down by being overly zealous. It can be overwhelming, and what you think is motivating is de-motivating. When I look back at me, I would have been scared to death to walk into a meeting with me. Because I thought I was being exciting. I thought I was being motivational. And as it turns out, being too exciting and too motivational is overbearing, and it turns people off. And so you've got to get to a level where you understand that. You've got to catch yourself. You think the music's so good you turn it up, but it can be so loud that they don't want to hear it."

Plumeri described how he learned the lesson.

"One of the problems with that kind of style is that there are very few people who want to tell you that there's something wrong with that," Plumeri said. "You know, you don't just walk in and say to somebody—you're a little noisy today, or a little bit over-bearing. I think you need to pay attention to people. I think one of the things that's important about my job—or any job where you have influence over people and you can make a difference—is you pay attention to people. You pay attention to their body language. You pay attention to how they're reacting to you. I remember a good friend also saying to me, 'You can be much better than you are.' And I said, 'What are you talking about?' And he said, 'You know, if you gave other people a chance to participate in what excites you, and have them get excited along with you, rather than you feeling like it's your responsibility to make sure they're excited all the time, you could really do some great stuff.' And that stuck with me. I don't mean to suggest that I've mastered that, and there's not a period at the end of that sentence. It's still a work in progress."

Deborah Dunsire of Millennium shared her story of learning how to step out of the sandbox, as she put it.

"When you desperately want to do well—and I am a person who's typically worked hard and done well—it's very important to me to be improving, to be good at what I do," Dunsire said. "Sometimes that desire in me translated into overdoing it on the leadership side, where if something went wrong, I thought I had to fix it personally. As I've stepped further and further outside of my comfort zone to the job I'm in now, which has the fullest breadth of the company, I've had to focus more on the work of leadership and not to focus on being the person who solved the details of the problem. Sometimes if something didn't go well, I would feel I had to get involved personally, in some ways duplicating what the person who worked for me was doing. I had to learn to step away from this, and ask myself what I could uniquely do. The focus on the work of leadership means asking yourself the questions, 'What do I add? What can I bring that that person cannot access without me?' Some of it is integrating across functions, for example. That's a resource I could bring.

"One lesson I had was from a particular person who graciously gave me semi-direct but quite gentle feedback that said, 'You're in my sandbox and we're not accomplishing a lot being in here together.' So that was helpful. Then I heard feedback from my team, which said, 'Gee, sometimes we know you're good at this stuff and you've done it, but sometimes we need to kind of bang our heads a little bit more without you fixing it.' So I learned to step away sometimes and in the right situation allow them to stub their toes. You don't allow them to do that if the chairman's coming for a presentation, but in a safe situation, to allow them to present their work with the flaw that you can see clearly because you've done this more times than they have, and letting them learn from that. It also came at a time when I was more confident in my own leadership, and that in allowing that to happen I wasn't failing. I learned to separate the fact that everything had to go perfectly for me in order to feel I was being the leader I needed to be. Also, as I grew, I understood more and more that the job of leadership is developing people and that it involves not doing everything for them, but sometimes allowing them to stub their toes. I'm a mum. You do this with your kids, too."

Dunsire also described how she had learned to pull back in meetings.

"Every strength taken to extreme becomes a weakness, right? So you have to manage your strengths effectively," she said. "One of my strengths came from my father, who used to, just for sport, engage in debates over the dinner table. So he would always take a position he knew would get a rise out of me, and he would engage in a debate, such as whether Communism was the right answer for the world. It might be something totally antithetical to what I knew his beliefs would be, and he would just go there, and I would take the bait. He taught me to argue a position and we would go at it, and he also taught me how to argue to win and just be relentless in building the argument until there was no room for the opposition. That helps you be very analytical, very logical, and very articulate .and succinct, which are all strengths. However, when you are dealing with someone, particularly with a more junior person who's presenting you a position, if there are flaws in the logic, believe me, I'll find them. That, as a peer to peer, is bad enough. When you're senior and the other person is more junior, it becomes inappropriate because it shuts down that person's ability to discuss. So, I learned to ask questions in a different way because the feedback I got was, it's like a laser—I just laser in on the flaws in the argument and start peeling them down and that feels very uncomfortable. I learned in a situation where the logic was just too flawed to simply say, 'You know, maybe this is not ready for prime time yet. We could look at these one or two things and we could look at this again in a week or a day, depending on the urgency.' And then I could have an offline conversation with that person's manager and get it out of a meeting situation, where the last thing you want to do is destroy somebody. I think that tendency of being able to argue and win would be better suited to a criminal courtroom than a business setting. There's nothing wrong with the strength of being able to do that. The trick is how you manage it in the situation you're in."

Alan Mulally of the Ford Motor Company said that he learned an important lesson about letting go of some control when he first became a manager at Boeing.

"I remember when I was promoted to be a supervisor," he said. "I was an engineer, and I was going to manage some engineers. It was associated with an airplane program. It was going to be exciting and fun. So, I had my thoughts about what that supervisory job should be. At the time, an engineer I supervised would prepare his work, and I would sign it and approve it. I thought that it was really important that it reflect my standards of quality, and so I helped this person get it done. And fourteen drafts later of his coordination sheet, he walked in and he quit. I said, 'Why are you quitting?' He said, 'Well, I think you're a great engineer and I think you'll be a good supervisor some day. But right now, this is just too much for me to be supervised this tightly.'

"It was a gem," Mulally said of this lesson. "Because I really thought about why it happened. I realized very early then that what I was really being asked to do was to help connect a set of talented people to a bigger goal, a bigger program, and help them move forward to even bigger contributions. And that was a different role from what was expected of me when I was expected to be a dynamite engineer. So, in a way, that early experience stayed with me forever about what it really means to be asked to supervise and what it really means to manage and lead."

Many executives said that one of their biggest challenges was learning to listen more.

"Over the years, something I really focus on is truly listening," said Teresa Taylor of Qwest Communications. "When I say that, I mean sometimes people act like they're listening but they're really formulating their own thoughts in their heads. I'm trying to put myself into someone else's shoes, trying to figure out what's motivating them, and why they are in the spot they're in."

Taylor said she learned that lesson through a number of experiences.

"In general, when I would get feedback along the way in my career, people would say you're not a very good listener," she said. "I would think I was, but everybody was telling me I wasn't. So I spent a lot of time, even in the earlier years, biting my lip, saying I've got to slow down and listen to what they're saying.

"When I came to Qwest, which was twenty-one years ago, I came into this very corporate structure, and every six months we do a review and at the end of the year you get rated. That's probably when it started, when someone wrote it down on a piece of paper, or checked a box that said, 'Need to work on listening.' So, because I thought I knew better, I probably ignored that for a good five years, and said, 'Oh, I know what I'm doing.' But as your responsibilities grow and as you're responsible for more departments and individuals and bigger initiatives and bigger budgets, you start paying attention to that.

"When you have smaller groups, you still are very hands-on, you still do a lot of the work. But it was when I reached a point where my department was so big I couldn't do all the work or I would have killed myself working 24/7. When I reached a point where there was no way to get it done except to influence through individuals, that's when I had to take a step back and say, 'Well, I can't muscle my way through this. I can't do it myself. I can't get through this. I'm working weekends and nights and I'm working crazy, and we're not getting anywhere, we're not getting the result.'

"I was very hands-on and redoing other people's work if it wasn't just the way I thought it should be. I would take it and change it on the weekend and say, 'Well, here's a better way.' That was earlier in my career, and I had a my-way-or-the-highway kind of approach. It was successful. I kept getting rewarded for it. You get a bigger job and bigger things, and then you reach the point where the job becomes so big that that doesn't work anymore. You got to where you were because you move quickly, you make decisions, you assess quickly, and you're rewarded for that. So by hitting your targets or your goals and getting it to happen, you get the next big job, and it keeps going. Then you get to a level where you can't touch all the work, you just can't. It's physically impossible because it's so large and so diverse. So then you say, 'I have to make sure I have the right people in place and they're motivated correctly, and the way to do that is to listen to them.' Otherwise, you'll be in a position where everything's filtered when it comes to you. So you have to dig under, and the only way to dig under is to listen. People have to believe you want to listen. Otherwise, you'll get the corporate gloss-over—everything's fine, don't worry."

By his own admission, Jeffrey Katzenberg of DreamWorks Animation spent a good part of his career as a micromanager.

"And if you talk about attributes that were my least good attributes, being a micromanager would certainly be on the top of my list," he confessed. Partly because of his age and job, he said he's evolved into a different kind of manager.

"Today there are several people within DreamWorks who are the students who became better than the teacher," he said. "I'm thrilled. I find myself getting completely comfortable with the idea that if somebody else can do my job as well as, let alone better than, I can, that's okay. Let me move on and find something else to do. What I have learned recently is to be a selective micromanager. There are times when it's actually good to be a micromanager, but mostly not."

He described the learning process.

"Just with time, the quality of the people around me impressed me," he said. "I started to realize that if I wanted to stay surrounded by great people, I had to get out of their way and create the room and make sure they started to get the recognition and the credit and everything that goes with it. Honestly, it allowed me to stay around longer."

He also learned when it's time to micromanage and when it's time to let go.

"It's an hourly process of when to get in and when not to and to know when it matters," he said. "One of the up-and-coming superstars who works with us is Bill Damaschke, who's the head creative guy at the studio. He said this amazing thing to me a couple years ago that has resonated with me day after day after day. He said, 'Jeffrey, different is not necessarily better.'

"So if an actor says a line in one particular way that I like and the director likes another way, my different idea isn't always better. Sometimes it is, but not always, and that's the thing Bill has made me really think about. When I have a reaction to something, now there's a five-second tape delay. I try to self-edit in that way if I can. For decades, I would always go first in meetings to discuss opinions on stories, a sequence, design, artwork, or a music score. I don't like to go first anymore. I actually like to hear what other people have to say first."

For Katzenberg, the core of that approach is respecting others.

"Being respectful of people, I think, is the single most important quality in leadership—earning the respect of people who work with you, for you, your customers, your investors," he said. "That to me is really what defines successful leadership—earning that respect. By definition if there's leadership, it means there are followers, and you're only as good as the followers. I believe the quality of the followers is in direct correlation to the respect you hold them in. It's not how much they respect you that is most important. It's actually how much you respect them. It's everything."

16.

CREATING A CULTURE

Every time a person walks into work, she makes a subconscious decision. How much of herself does she check at the front door? How much of her self-image, her sense of herself—who she is, who she wants to become, her hopes and dreams—is she going to leave outside? Does she say to herself, "This is just a job, it's a paycheck," and grit her teeth to put up with work to which she feels little connection? Perhaps she's become jaded by what she sees as favoritism, double standards, or ever-shifting rules based on the mood of the boss that day. She shuts down, folds her arms, and stares at the table in meetings to avoid making eye contact. She doesn't want to engage because she sees no point. She's grown cynical over months and years of watching top executives make boneheaded decisions.

One of the running jokes in the famous cartoon strip *Calvin and Hobbes* was an imaginary game called "Calvinball" that young

Calvin played with his stuffed animal, Hobbes. They make up new rules at every moment. "The only permanent rule in Calvinball is that you can't play it the same way twice," Calvin explains in one strip. That may be fun if you're a kid, but does that remind you of some place you've worked, where you could never quite figure out the rules because the people in charge seemed to make them up anew every day?

One of the most demanding aspects of leadership is to create a positive culture that engages employees at a personal level. Even when you create a company from scratch, it can be hard, as Tony Hsieh of Zappos recalls about an early experience as an entrepreneur.

"After college, a roommate and I started a company called Link-Exchange in 1996, and it grew to about a hundred or so people, and then we ended up selling the company to Microsoft in 1998," Hsieh said. "From the outside, it looked like it was a great acquisition, $265 million, but most people don't know the real reason why we ended up selling the company. It was because the company culture just went completely downhill. When it was starting out, when it was just five or ten of us, it was like your typical dot-com. We were all really excited, working around the clock, sleeping under our desks, had no idea what day of the week it was. But we didn't know any better and didn't pay attention to company culture.

"By the time we got to a hundred people, even though we hired people with the right skill sets and experiences, I dreaded getting out of bed in the morning and was hitting that snooze button over and over again. I just didn't look forward to going to the office. The passion and excitement were no longer there. That's kind of a weird feeling for me because this was a company I co-founded, and if I was feeling that way, how must the other employees feel? That's actually why we ended up selling the company. For me, I didn't want to be part of a company where I dreaded going into the office."

Every company—even different departments of companies—can be like its own country, with its unique customs and culture. That culture is partly the product of the people who work there, and the infinite shadings of interactions that result when you bring a certain group of people together. But it is mostly a product of leadership. Creating an effective culture is an art, and in the bottom-line, results-driven world of business, culture can be relegated to the backseat, an afterthought filed under nice-but-not-necessary.

Many CEOs, however, recognize that culture is the engine that drives results, and that by creating the kind of culture where people want to come to work—and where they don't check a good portion of themselves at the door—the company can generate exceptional results and outperform competitors.

"I have a very simple model to run a company," said Stephen Sadove of Saks. "It starts with leadership at the top, which drives a culture. Culture drives innovation and whatever else you're trying to drive within a company—innovation, execution, whatever it's going to be. And that then drives results. When I talk to Wall Street, people really want to know your results, what are your strategies, what are the issues, what it is that you're doing to drive your business. They're focused on the bottom line. Never do you get people asking about the culture, about leadership, about the people in the organization. Yet, it's the reverse, because it's the people, the leadership, the culture, and the ideas that are ultimately driving the numbers and the results. So it's a flip. What I try to teach people is, don't ask the first question in terms of numbers. Let's talk about the people, let's talk about the culture, let's talk about the ideas and the innovation."

The Flatter, the Better

It's very easy for an organization to have its collective compass pointed at the boss in the corner office. It's human nature. People start asking the boss what he thinks all the time, and if he weighs in, then more decisions are passed up to him for approval. It can feed on itself pretty quickly, and suddenly there's a line of people outside the door asking for a decision rather than making it themselves. After all, if the boss wants this instead of that, then nobody except him can be blamed if it turns out to be the wrong choice.

Some of the most successful CEOs have taken steps—symbolic and practical—to create a culture that is less hierarchical, where people can make decisions themselves and learn from one another. In these organizations, CEOs become facilitators of the culture rather than the focus of the culture.

Vineet Nayar of HCL Technologies took some dramatic steps to push the focus away from his corner office.

"If you see your job not as chief strategy officer and the guy who has all the ideas but rather as the guy who is obsessed with enabling employees to create value, I think you will succeed," he said. "My job is to make sure everybody is enabled to do what they do well.

"You have to create a culture of pushing the envelope of trust. How do we push the envelope of trust? By creating transparency. All HCL's financial performance information is on our internal Web site. We are completely open. We put all the dirty linen on the table, and we answer everyone's questions on that Web site. We inverted the pyramid of the organization and made reverse accountability a reality.

"I'll give you one more example with the way we handle business planning. So, what is the absolute power of the CEO? You come and make a presentation to me about what you're going to do, and I will sit in this chair God has given to me and tell you if I like the plan or not. The power of the hierarchy flows from the fact that I will comment on what you write. As my kids became teenagers, I started looking at Facebook a little more closely. It was a significant amount of collaboration. There was open understanding. They didn't have a problem sharing their status. Nothing seemed to be secret, and they were living their lives very openly, and friends were commenting on each other and it was working. Here is my generation, which is very security-conscious and privacy-conscious, and I thought, what are the differences? This is the generation coming to work for us. It's not my generation.

"So we started having people make their presentations and record them for our internal Web site. We open that for review to a 360-degree workshop, which means your subordinates will review it. Your managers will read it. Your peers will read it, and everybody will comment on it. I will be, or your manager will be, one of the many who read it. So every presentation was reviewed by three hundred, four hundred people.

"What happened? There were two very interesting lessons I learned. One, because your subordinates are going to see the plan, you cannot lie. You have to be honest. Two, because your peers are going to see it, you are going to put your best work into it. Third, you didn't learn from me. You learned by reviewing somebody else's presentation. You learned from the comments somebody else gave you. For the eight thousand people who participated, a massive collaborative learning took place."

Building a culture of collaboration is a priority for Cristóbal Conde of SunGard.

"Collaboration is one of the most difficult challenges in management," he said. "I think top-down organizations got started because the bosses either knew more or they had access to more information. None of that applies now. Everybody has access to identical amounts of information.

"With the explosion of information, I think that a CEO needs to focus more on the platform that enables collaboration, because employees already have all the data. They have access to everything. You have to work on the structure of collaboration. How do people get recognized? How do you establish a meritocracy in a highly dispersed environment?

"The answer is to allow employees to develop a name for themselves that is irrespective of their organizational ranking or where they sit in the org chart. And it actually is not a question about monetary incentives. They do it because recognition from their peers is, I think, an extremely strong motivating factor, and something that is broadly unused in modern management.

"One thing we use is a Twitter-like system on our intranet called Yammer. By having technologies that allow people to see what others are doing, share information, collaborate, brag about their successes—that is what flattens the organization. I think the role of the boss is to then work on those collaboration platforms, as opposed to being the one making the decisions. It's more like the producer of the show rather than being the lead. I think too many bosses think that their job is to be the lead, and I don't. By creating an atmosphere of collaboration, the people who are consistently right get a huge following, and their work product is talked about by people they've never met. It's fascinating."

The point is to get people talking to each other rather than always trying to involve the CEO in every decision. Some CEOs push back when employees try to delegate decision-making up.

Kasper Rorsted, the CEO of Henkel, a consumer and industrial products company based in Düsseldorf, has a simple policy to keep pushing decision-making down: he tells everyone at the company that he doesn't read "cc" e-mails—those where he is copied but is not intended as the main reader.

"If they want to write to me, they can write to me," he said. "If not, it's very often to cover your back and they need to deal with their business and I need to deal with my business. I mean if it's important, they need to write it to me, but I'm not going to read an e-mail for cc. I just don't do it. I delete it."

Daniel Amos of Aflac also pushes back when people ask him to make a decision they should be making. "My theory is that when you start telling people what to do, they no longer are responsible; you are. I'll give them my opinion and say; 'Look, this is my opinion, but if you choose that and you fail, you're not blaming it on me. It is your fault.' I think it makes them stronger."

What Are Our Values?

Ideally, values in a corporation act as a guide to help make tough decisions. When there are shades of gray, and there are always many shades of gray in difficult calls, values can help frame the discussion. What do we believe in? What's really important to us over the long haul? Values also appeal to employees who want a sense of mission beyond dollars and cents.

Values get a lot of lip service in corporate America. A booming cottage industry stands at the ready to help companies draw up mission statements. Signs are made. Cards are laminated. And they are often quickly forgotten.

Other CEOs dig a little harder to establish values, and reinforce their importance by constantly talking about values as the guiding principles for decisions large and small. They make sure that the company abides by the rules reflected in the values, because they know that once a gap starts emerging between talk and actions, people will roll their eyes and stop paying attention.

There is no one way to develop these value systems. Some CEOs have established them themselves. Others have let their staffs develop them on their own. Another approach is for the CEO to guide the process and provide input, or hire consultants to come in and facilitate the discussion. The point is that it's not the process that matters as much as clarity and commitment. Employees can adapt to different value systems, just as people can play all sorts of different sports and games. Do the values make sense? Are they really used as the guiding principles to help make tough decisions, or are they discarded at a moment's notice? Does it feel like another round of Calvinball?

"We asked ourselves, 'What are the values going to be that are going to guide this agency?'" said Sharon Napier of Partners + Napier. "They started out as seven, but the three that are on the wall when you walk into our office are *courage, ingenuity,* and *family.* The family one is really interesting to me because I ended up getting my M.B.A. at forty-five years old. And one of the professors said to me, 'How are you going to grow your company with a family value?' It made me really think. I thought about it as mutual respect: 'I've got your back. We're going to create a family. We're going to cover for each other.' We're three times as big since then, so he was wrong. I think people have to come to work every day and have something that's part of their DNA, something that helps them make decisions, and so I think that was really important, and it has really shaped my leadership."

At Zappos, the company tells employees that values are not just suggestions—they can be used as grounds for dismissal if employees aren't abiding by them.

"At Zappos, we view culture as our number-one priority," Tony Hsieh said. "We decided that if we get the culture right, most of the stuff, like building a brand around delivering the very best customer service, will just take care of itself. About five years ago, we formalized the definition of our culture into ten core values. We wanted to come up with committable core values, meaning that we would actually be willing to hire and fire people based on those values, regardless of their individual job performance. Given those criteria, it's actually pretty tough to come up with core values.

"We spent a year doing that. I basically sent out an e-mail to the entire company, asking what our values should be, and got a whole bunch of different responses. The initial list was actually thirty-seven long, and then we ended up condensing and combining and went back and forth and came up with our list of ten. Honestly, there was a lot of resistance to the core values rolling out, including from me. I was very hesitant, because it felt like one of those big-company things to do. But within a couple of months, it just made such a huge difference. It gave everyone a common language, and created a lot more alignment in terms of how everyone in the company was thinking.

"Today, we actually do two separate sets of interviews. The hiring manager and his or her team will interview for the standard fit within the team, relevant experience, technical ability, and so on. But then our HR department does a separate set of interviews purely for culture fit. They actually have questions for each and every one of the core values. Some of them are behavioral questions. One of our values is, "Create fun and a little weirdness." So one of our interview questions is, literally, on a scale of 1 to 10, how weird are you? If you're a 1, you're probably a little bit too straitlaced for us. If you're a 10, you might be too psychotic for us.

"It's not so much the number; it's more seeing how candidates react to a question. Because our whole belief is that everyone is a little weird somehow, so it's really more a fun way of saying that we recognize and celebrate each person's individuality, and we want their true personalities to shine in the workplace environment, whether it's with co-workers or when talking with customers."

Zappos pushes the culture of transparency to an extreme that might make some companies uncomfortable. It publishes a "culture book" every year. Hsieh explained the process: "We ask all our employees to write a few paragraphs about what the Zappos culture means to them and, except for typos, it's unedited, so you get to read the good and bad. It's kind of like customer reviews you might read on Web sites, but these are essentially employee reviews of the company and our culture. We make it freely available to visitors and anybody who asks for a copy."

At Zappos, ideas for values were solicited from the staff. At The Container Store, they came mostly from the founder, Kip Tindell.

"I studied a lot of philosophy at Jesuit High School in Dallas," he said. "One of the things that really struck me was that most people seem to think that there's a separate code of conduct in business from your personal life. And I always believed they should be the same. So we have what we call foundation principles. They are talked about and emphasized around here constantly. They're all almost corny, a little bit Golden Rule-ish, but it causes two things. It causes everybody to act as a unit. Even though we're sort of liberating everybody to choose the means to the ends, we all agree on the ends, and the foundation principles are what cause us to agree on the ends. As a result, we have people unshackled to choose any means to those ends, but it's not mayhem because our foundation principles kind of tie us together. When I was a kid, I was put in leadership roles early on, and throughout the time I was growing up I began to keep a file of thoughts that I believed were the best thoughts I'd ever heard, and those became more and more business-oriented as time went on.

"In the early days of The Container Store, we of course had so much closeness with each employee, we were so small, that if you were managing someone and you were having trouble with them, all you really had to do was go out to eat a meal with them, and then you could kind of straighten it all out. You could talk about it. And that becomes much more difficult to do as the organization becomes larger and you don't have as much direct contact and as much time to just talk about things. When we opened the Houston store in 1988, it was so busy we couldn't keep up with anything. It was three or four times the business level we had ever experienced before. We were hiring people who were not appropriate culture fits. We were just hiring anybody. It was a nightmare. It was like a different business. It wasn't the same culture or the same customer service level. So there wasn't any leadership going on.

"Anyway, we literally didn't know what to do about it, so we called a meeting of all the employees at the store manager's home. I actually wanted to be a good leader. I wanted to be inspirational. I wanted to be able to communicate to them what we were lacking here and how we could get it. And that was when I dipped into that file of all the best thoughts I'd ever heard in my life and found the ones that represented the way we did business, though they had never been written down before. We thought this and we thought that, but they had never been communicated before. I thought they would think they were corny or I thought they'd start throwing fruit at me or something.

"It was just amazing, and all anybody wanted me to do for months was just go around and talk about the foundation principles and how we apply them to our company, and how that makes us cohesive and act as a team, act as a unit. And I began to see the incredible fierce pride that people had working for a company that believed all these things. When you start a business you have a very fortunate thing in that you have the opportunity to mold a business around your philosophy, and that's a very cool thing."

Fair's Fair

Few things drain energy faster from a workforce than a sense that there's a double standard, an inside track that they're missing out on. People might get promoted over more capable colleagues, or underperforming workers can seem protected, getting the same pay and rewards as those who are working harder. Many CEOs try to create a culture of fairness, and to minimize the politics that can consume an organization.

"I think it's a real cliché to say that the boss is the one that sets the tone, but it's absolutely true," said Cristóbal Conde of Sun-Gard. "In most companies where there are politics, it's because the boss starts most of it and pits people against each other and doesn't communicate and doesn't treat peers equally. The boss allows for the informal organization chart to be very different from the formal organization chart. I think people watch your actions, and they watch most of all when somebody gets fired. Because it's not the words of the mission statement or the words on the value statement, it's how a company deals with the people who breach the core values. That's what really defines the values; it's the exceptions."

Conde said one of his goals is to create a "frictionless" organization so that there are as few distractions as possible, and people can focus on the work.

"It starts by making yourself, as the boss, behave the way you want the rest of the organization to behave, and to an extreme degree," he said. "I never raise my voice. I happen to think that people who raise their voices can't listen when they're talking very loud. So I speak very quietly and, soon enough, everybody else starts speaking quietly.

"I also think by having very clear goals and clear compensation schemes, people don't feel that they need to be talking about compensation or about their bonus. It really does start by setting the tone from the top, and then it filters down. Now, it doesn't necessarily filter everywhere, because, in any organization, middle management seems to live by its own rules. But you can dramatically impact the way two levels down behave."

Kevin Sharer of Amgen sent a forceful signal to his new management team when he became CEO to make it clear that playing politics was only going to hurt them, not help them.

"I remember when the new team was assembled, having a dinner and sitting around the table, and I said, 'You know, we're new, we're together, we all feel lucky to be here, but let me tell you something. I've operated in environments where there were master politicians. I'm not a bad politician myself. And so I can see it. And if any of you try to be politicians, I will know it, and I will fire you.' We laugh about that now as a table-setting meeting and I think it stuck."

Mark Pincus of Zynga has established an unusual rule at his company—people can switch teams to work for a different manager if they choose. The point is to establish a culture of fairness, a meritocracy where people are rewarded for performance.

"The only way people will have the trust to give their all to their job is if they feel like their contribution is recognized and valued," he said. "And if they see somebody else higher than they are just because of a good résumé, or they see somebody else promoted who they don't think deserves it, you're done. My approach is that you have to earn the respect of people you work with. And so, if you come in and you start bossing people around and they don't want to work with you, they won't. In our company, if you want to switch teams, you can."

Sharon Napier of Partners + Napier has established a culture at her company of people earning promotions by doing the work first, then earning the title, so that everybody collectively nods in approval when somebody officially moves up.

"We always say when we promote somebody that we hope people say, 'It's about time'—that people have already been following that person, and so organically he or she has gotten to the next level," she said. "Then we acknowledge it with a promotion."

"You can watch and see people following them. You can walk around the office and they're running an agency meeting, or they have already decided that there's this meeting with the client and they're going to do this after. They're always thinking beyond what their task is. We have a creative director who just got moved to a vice president, and when we announced it at the agency meeting it was kind of, 'Well, it's about time. She's been doing that forever.' We love that because you've earned the respect and trust of your peers and your clients. It's not some arbitrary thing that's given."

Get People to Open Up

At Partners + Napier, all new hires have to introduce themselves to the entire agency, including those who are joining the monthly meeting via teleconference. It sets a tone that the company wants to know who you are as a person, not just that you're going to fill a role. But it's not just a matter of saying, "Hi, my name is . . ." New employees are expected to perform.

"They can get up and do absolutely anything they want for five minutes," said Sharon Napier. "Some will sing. Some will do a skit. Some will bake cookies and talk about when they were baking these cookies they were writing a blog, and here's all the things they were thinking about. Or here are the ten things you should know about me. They are incredibly creative."

At Kimpton Hotels and Restaurants, new managers have to participate in a hula hoop competition.

"One of the important aspects of working at Kimpton is having fun," said Niki Leondakis. "For leaders, the ability to laugh at yourself is key, so we use hula hoops to demonstrate that. Every year at our annual meeting, we have a general-manager meeting. About 250 people, along with our corporate team, get together for a couple of days. This has been a ritual for about fifteen years now. Anyone who's a first-timer we call up to the front of the room, and we play the music to 'Wipe Out,' and we do this 'hoop-off.' So five people at a time hoop and then there's a winner. There are usually four to six new teams of people. The winner of all the newbies, as we call them, then has a hoop-off with last year's reigning champion."

Jeffrey Swartz of Timberland will draw people out—with a bit of good-natured teasing—at new-hire orientations to deliver a message about the culture of his company.

"I go to every new-employee thing, and I do a warm-up exercise," Swartz said. "I say to folks, 'We'll start with a hard question, which is, what is your name? There's an HR person in the room. If you're not sure and you get nervous, just look over there and she'll remind you of your name. And having said your name, say your favorite place in the outdoors.'

"And instantly you'll see people's memories, visual memory, whatever. And I say, 'Hey, just to remind you, the HR person doesn't have that one written down, so you can say Niagara Falls or the Grand Canyon or anything else you want to say and no one's going to call you on it, so please, there's low pressure on this.'

"And so you go around the room and people say things. It's very cute. There was one woman, and you'd think her head's going to explode, and she goes: 'All right. Now I'll admit it. I don't belong here. My favorite place is not a hiking trail. It's not a mountain. I love Manhattan. I love the smell of it.' And I said, 'Okay, good.' And she was like, 'All right, I'm a failure.' And I said, 'No, listen.' And then I have this little standard speech that I say to people. 'I asked you your name because it wasn't your résumé we hired, it was you. It wasn't your brother. It wasn't your sister. It wasn't the person who sits next to you at the company that you came from. It was you. The individual matters. Two, I asked you about your favorite place in the outdoors. And so I reinforced the fact that it's all about you. But then if you noticed, everybody had someplace to say because we're trying to serve this notion of outdoor spirit.' It's kind of cool, because while the individual experience matters, look how universally held it is. Even when people say the same beach, which every once in a while they do, they have a very different experience of the beach, of that same beach. So, in hiring, I'm desperately probing for the human inside the shell because the people who succeed at Timberland show a little leg, meaning they expose themselves. You have to. To go to a company town-hall meeting and call out to question a strategy you don't understand or a deeply felt thing, you've got to show up.

"You know the line in *The Godfather*—'Nothing personal. It's just business.' At Timberland, I want to make it clear from the beginning it is personal. Not invasive-personal, like I need to know what's going on in your life. But if you aren't going to play at the level of personal, it's probably not going to be nourishing for either of us.

"A willingness to be exposed, a willingness to acknowledge the personal dimension, a willingness to value the personal dimension—from the beginning, that's what we're after. I'm saying that there's no chance that our company, in a cruddy industry in a world that's in an L-shaped recession, not a V- or a W-shaped recession, is going to be able to reinvent itself with the speed and ease that it needs to unless we bring more than our intellects to the table."

Workers can easily get stuck in comfort zones, talking to the same people. Sheila Marcelo of Care.com established a policy to guard against that: she moves everyone to a new desk once a year, and she assigns the seats.

"People don't have a choice where they sit," she said. "Part of the reason was to embrace change, to remove turfiness so that you're not just chatting with your friends and sitting with your friends. You sit with somebody else from a different team so you get to know their job. What are they doing? What are they saying on the phone? How do they tick? And it's getting to know different people so that we build a really big team. And we do that every year. And it's now actually become an exciting thing that people embrace."

Challenge, Don't Criticize

A group has gathered for a meeting, and someone ventures an opinion. Another person takes issue with the idea and questions it. Does the person who started the exchange get his back up and push back because he's taken the questioning as criticism? Or does he take it as the first step in a healthy debate, knowing that the idea will be improved by argument?

The difference speaks volumes about the kind of company people work in, and the tone is set at the top. Does the CEO, as a role model, encourage healthy debate and appreciate tough questions and challenges? Or does she set a my-way-or-the-highway rule? Either one will inevitably filter down through the organization. If a manager can create a culture where challenges are welcomed and encouraged as constructive feedback, and simply part of pressure-testing an idea to make sure it holds up, then she will have scored an important victory in getting her employees to commit more of themselves to the organization. If employees sense that their opinions are not welcomed and will not be heard, then they will start checking more of themselves at the front door when they walk into work.

"It's important to get people to challenge and question each other without taking offense, to set a tone in an organization where people can do this comfortably, that they understand it's not just about them," said Ursula Burns of Xerox, who has talked to her employees about overcoming what she described as the company's "terminal niceness."

The culture within the company has for decades been referred to as the "Xerox family" because of the loyalty that employees have to the company, a place filled with long-term veterans. Burns herself grew up in a family where her mother was frank and blunt and had high expectations of her daughter. Burns wanted to infuse that spirit in the company a bit more.

"When we're in the family, you don't have to be as nice as when you're outside of the family," she explained at a large gathering of her employees. "I want us to stay civil and kind, but we have to be frank—and the reason we can be frank is because we are all in the same family." Nods of recognition rippled across the audience. "We know it. We know what we do," she continued, describing meetings where some people present and others just listen. "And then the meeting ends, and we leave and say, 'Man, that wasn't true.' I'm like, 'Why didn't you say that in the meeting?'"

At AdMob, meetings are all about challenging the status quo and questioning what's wrong and what can be done better, said Omar Hamoui.

"We spend a great amount of time talking about everything that's wrong. Not because we're trying to be negative. You can only talk for so long about what's going well and have it be useful. You can be a lot more productive if you spend time on the things that aren't going well. When visitors came to our board meetings, I would have to spend time prepping them ahead of time, basically telling them, 'Don't worry. The company's not falling apart. Everything's going fine. This is just how we are.'

"It just means that nobody at AdMob is shy to point out a problem or an issue with a product or service, even if it's a product or service they didn't build or they don't own or doesn't fall within their domain. People aren't shy about bringing up these issues and being fairly demanding that we solve them. I think that that's led to us being very proactive. We're just very, very upfront about those things."

Jen-Hsun Huang of Nvidia said "intellectual honesty" is one of the core values of his company.

"It's the ability to call a spade a spade, to as quickly as possible recognize that we've made a mistake, that we've gone the wrong way, and that we learn from it and quickly adjust," Huang said. "Without intellectual honesty, you can't have a culture that's willing to tolerate failure because people cling too much to an idea that likely will be bad or isn't working and they feel like their reputation is tied up in it. They can't admit failure. You end up putting too much into a bad idea and then you risk the entire enterprise. And I like people who are able to call a spade a spade. If something is right, something's right. If something's wrong, something's wrong. And if something could be better, it could be better."

William Green of Accenture has tried to create a culture of coaching and healthy debate throughout his organization.

"One of our other principles is that people who are successful are the ones who ask for help," he said. "It sounds simple, but to get an organization to believe that asking for help is a sign of strength, and not weakness, is a huge thing. It's easy to judge and criticize. Anyone can do that, and you'll get nothing. I say to our organization, 'I don't have any time for criticism, but you can challenge me all day long.' The distinction is really simple, and it's criticism that causes people to raise their defenses, and challenging people causes them to raise their game. If you lead an organization and you just challenge people to be better, they will blow away what you think they're capable of doing. That's a state of mind, and somewhere along the line, I had a chance to recognize the distinction between the two.

"It's like learning. With a motivated learner, you can work wonders. In institutions, it's the same thing. Are there companies with the will and resolve to change? That's the equivalent of a motivated learner. Or are there companies that are just sort of stuck where they are, and they like the status quo? In the end, that's the difference between winners and losers in corporate America and around the world. That's the contrast."

Reward It

As David Novak of Yum Brands explained in chapter 14, "Small Gestures, Big Payoffs," people typically leave their companies for one of two reasons. One is that they don't get along with the boss. The second is that they don't feel their efforts are appreciated. Some CEOs make sure that people are rewarded in ways beyond their paychecks.

"I bring all of the U.S. employees together every two months," said Michael Mathieu of YuMe. "I want to tell them how we're doing, what's on my mind, and recognize people who've exhibited the leadership characteristics that we foster at YuMe. We give out an award, and that particular employee has it until the next vote. Then they hand it to the person who wins it next. People vote for the person who best epitomizes my mantra, which is: Be passionate about what you do and be interested in making the people around you better. These people show humility. They're selfless. They will work for other people's success. The people who win are the ones who are the most team-oriented. They're not the ones who have the best skills. But they're passionate about what they do. They're a positive influence. They're not in the lunchroom gossiping about somebody. That's one of my tenets. If you have issues with a colleague, go to your colleague and say, 'Joe, this is what I'm thinking.' Have a candid conversation."

Omar Hamoui of AdMob has established a memorable way for the group to reward itself for a big victory—using a gong.

"The most common feedback I got was that I needed to be more positive and praise people more when things are going well. It's fine to make people comfortable with talking about what's negative, but if you yourself aren't really acknowledging the good things, that tends to eventually wear on people.

"One of the other things we did based on that feedback was we got this giant gong. It ended up becoming a pretty important part of the culture for anything good that was happening. There'll just be a note that goes out to the entire office. We get everybody in the room, and then we will gong, and we'll say, 'We launched this new product,' 'We did this big sale,' or 'We got this big deal.' It became a really, really important part of our culture. It definitely became a nice symbol of the things that were going well.

"There's sort of a collective intelligence about what's gong-worthy because you don't want to assemble everybody to talk about something that is commonplace. We had a gong when we hit our ten-billionth ad, then we had another gong when we hit our hundred-billionth ad. But we didn't gong every ten billion along the way. It has to be special. We do have one epic gong, which is the triple gong, which is if something completely monumental happens, you hit the gong three times in a row. It gets louder and louder each time. That we reserve for only very special occasions."

Use Fresh Eyes

Bringing in a new hire provides a new set of eyes on a corporate culture. Some CEOs use them to get a fresh perspective.

"I think some of the best ideas come from people who aren't stuck in their ways," said Stephen Sadove of Saks. "I always tell people new to my organization when they come in, 'I want you, in your first three or four weeks, to jot down every time you have an idea or a question about how things are done, and then stick it in your drawer. Just whatever it is, why are we doing it this way? I don't care whether it's good or bad; I don't want you to even talk to anyone about it. Just write it down and stick it in the drawer. And at the end of three or four weeks I want you to look at the sheet. Maybe you'll say, "Now, I understand that. Now it makes a little bit of sense to me." Or you may look at it and say, "That still doesn't make any sense to me." Then I want you to sit with me and we're going to talk about them.' Invariably, I find some really good ideas that make you say, 'Why are we doing it this way? It makes no sense at all.' I've seen little things, big things, waste in the system, and a lot of duplication of work. Things like that come out of it."

Linda Heasley, the CEO of The Limited, will debrief new

managers after three months. During that period, she asks them to watch and listen, and to resist the feeling that they have to prove themselves and have an immediate impact.

"I tell them: 'Take ninety days. The relationships you build in your first few months here are critical to your success. Try not to talk in meetings. I know you're going to want to demonstrate that you're really capable and you deserve to be here by showing your smarts. But if you listen and let the void fill with what's around you, you'll learn a ton.'

"It's really important to take the ninety days and watch and listen, and it's really hard to do that, because people want to perform out of the gate. It's great for me, because I get new eyes telling me what they've seen. It's always interesting for me to hear how newcomers feel after they've been in the brand for a period of time and to get feedback. Is there something we should be thinking about doing differently?"

17.

SO WHAT IS LEADERSHIP?

It may be one of the ultimate fill-in-the-blank questions, right up there with "What is the meaning of life?" and "What are the secrets to happiness?" And just as with those questions, there are many right answers. Out of the infinite set of variables that make up successful leadership, it's always possible to point to two things, or twenty things, and proclaim them to be the keys, the secrets, the safe-cracking code.

But leadership is not that simple, because learning to lead requires making sense of a unique mix of a particular leader's personality, the organization she's running, the challenges she's facing at any given moment, and the personalities of the people she manages. Even trying to rank leadership principles is of little use, since the most important lesson for one person may be old hat for another. People learn to lead through experience; there really are no shortcuts. But CEOs who have learned to lead can, like high-altitude sherpas, offer some guidance about how to handle the challenges along the way.

For all the practical advice that CEOs can offer, it is still a fair question: *So what is leadership?* What are the intangibles that serve as a kind of connective tissue for all the skills of leadership— including the five qualities described in Part One—and help make a person a leader at his core?

Unbridled Passion for What's Possible

Many people are adept at making the most of the facts at hand, the current circumstances. Leaders have something extra: a gut sense for what's missing, where the opportunities are—a kind of confident, purposeful optimism about what's possible. They have ideas, even if those ideas are broad-brush and vague, about where their organization can go and what it can accomplish. They may not have a detailed road map, but they have inklings, a sparkle in their eyes, that inspire confidence and a collective sense of ambition.

Dan Rosensweig of Chegg said he learned this lesson from some of the famous entrepreneurs he's worked for.

"One of the blessings I've had, for my entire career, is working with founders of companies, whether it was Bill Ziff at Ziff Davis or with Jerry Yang and David Filo at Yahoo," he said. "What I love about that culture is the energy, enthusiasm, and the unbridled passion for what's possible, as opposed to spending a whole lot of time trying to figure out the obstacles.

"In Silicon Valley, if you spend a lot of time thinking about the obstacles, you'll talk yourself out of everything, because the more you look at it, the less logical something sounds, since no one has done it yet. Founders simply ask what needs to be done and what's the best way to do it. And that's fun. It's had a significant impact on the way I think, the way I lead, the way I manage, and the opportunities I seek out.

"I like being surrounded by people who have very little fear and very little respect for the past—not in a negative way, but in a positive way. They appreciate everything that's been done, but they constantly look for how to do it better. When you lead with what's possible, and how you create value for people, it's energizing. Being around that kind of energy and inspiration has allowed me to think bigger than I probably ever would have thought."

Andrew Cosslett of InterContinental Hotels Group described the quality that helped him rally the sports teams he captained when he was younger, even when they seemed to be facing long odds.

"I've always been very positive and confident, and I guess that goes back a long way," he said. "I'm highly competitive, but I'm also very relaxed with people, and that combination makes people feel quite happy to be part of my team. I can talk about changing things for the better, even if I don't know what it is we're going to change. I'll just say we're going over there somewhere. And I don't quite know what that looks like, but it's going to be fantastic. And on the way we'll love what we're doing, have some laughs and a few beers, and it's going to be okay. And I'm going to make you really happy that I turned up and sat next to you, and we went on this journey together."

It's easy for anybody to make bold promises and brash claims. But why does a line of followers form behind some leaders, while others have trouble winning people over? George Barrett of Cardinal Health said that employees have to trust a visionary leader before they will follow him.

"Trust has a couple of dimensions," Barrett said. "It starts with competence. People have to believe that you really know what you're doing. They have to really trust your judgment because the data are so complex out there that they have to believe you can see through all the silliness and have some sense of the right course.

"People have to trust that you have a point of view about what this enterprise is going to look like. What do we seek to be? And they have to trust that you understand them, that you get them. Not necessarily that you know them personally, but you understand what it's all about to work here and that you have their interests at heart. I think that when you can do those things, it can be a powerful combination. I think people sometimes equate leadership with charisma and decisiveness. I think those are powerful tools, and I hope I have both, but they're not to be confused with leadership. I know a lot of very charismatic people who lack judgment and competence, and they're not great leaders. They're just fun to be around. And I know some very decisive people who lack judgment, which is terrifying."

Build a Story Around Their Capabilities

Effective managers, like good coaches, can make people better at their jobs. But leaders also have a feel, an instinct, for what people are capable of becoming, even if they can't see it themselves. They see the best in a person, and know how to bring out those strengths or shore up the weaknesses. They see possibilities for new jobs, new careers, paths for development to help that person. They know what's best for her, and they want what's best for her. Leaders who are committed to helping the people who work for them will have committed followers.

"I think as the years have gone on, I've really honed my ability to listen and understand everybody's story, and to help them build a story around their capabilities—a story that's open-ended, that plays to their strengths," said James Rogers of Duke Energy. "One of the biggest things I find in organizations is that people tend to limit their perceptions of themselves and their capabilities, and one of my challenges is to open them up to the possibilities. I have this belief that anybody can do almost anything in the right context.

"Oftentimes, I do it by moving people around in the organization and putting them in areas where they're uncomfortable. There are clearly role players. But you have to push some people out of their comfort zone. You've got to have a sense of individuals, that they're willing to take on that risk, because if you try to push them and you sense they don't want to go there, then it's probably a mistake. And so it's more art than science, it's more feel. That's what I'm better at, the longer I've been CEO—I understand when no is no and no is maybe. I think that, at the end of the day, they have to trust you. They have to trust that you wouldn't be asking them to do this unless you had confidence in them. They have to trust that you see something in them that they may not see completely in themselves. So I think it really gets down to them trusting me. I tell them, 'I'm confident you can do it, but I want you to know I'm here for you, I've got your back, and at the end of the day, I'm going to help you succeed because I know you can.'"

David Novak of Yum Brands has a similar philosophy of leadership:

"The best leaders I've known really take an active interest in a person. And once that person demonstrates they have skill and capability, they try to help them achieve their potential. That's always been my thinking about management. If you have someone who's smart, talented, aggressive, and wants to learn, then your job is to help them become all they can be. What I think a great leader does, a great coach does, is understand what kind of talent you have and then help leverage that talent so that people can achieve what they never thought they were capable of. The only way you can do that is to care about the people who work for you. No one's going to care about you unless you care about them. But if you care about someone, genuinely, then they're going to care about you because you're making a commitment and an investment in them."

Bringing the Group Together

In many quarters, CEOs are seen as two-dimensional figures, driven by money, greed, a lust for fame, and perhaps an overzealous sense of competition. View them through the lens of their pay packages and it's easy for skepticism to turn to cynicism, particularly because of the gap that often exists between pay and performance. Many aspects of executive compensation remain flawed.

And while money is no doubt an important reward that drives many executives, it falls far short in explaining what motivates CEOs, many of whom spoke at length about their leadership philosophies. They ended up in the corner office not because they chased it, but because they performed like leaders and were promoted for that. The ability to bring a team together to achieve a goal is a rare skill, and CEOs are often rewarded handsomely for it. While the history of corporate America is filled with egomaniacal bosses, command-and-control leadership won't cut it in a world where the real competition is for talent.

"It's not culturally relevant anymore," said Mindy Grossman of HSN. "Even if you look at generations who are coming up, the notion of needing somebody to tell you what to do is not our culture. What happens with that sort of manager or CEO is that you're not going to keep intelligent, inspired talent, because they want some form of entrepreneurial capability to be able to exercise their talent. I want to challenge them to be able to do that. A second point is that all organizations are significantly diverse today, in terms of where people came from and how they grew up. We don't have as many command-and-control households anymore. Those aren't the cultures people want to be in."

Many CEOs see their role as enabling a culture to prosper, rather than being the focus of it.

"I think of myself less as a leader," said Tony Hsieh of Zappos, "and more of being almost an architect of an environment that enables employees to come up with their own ideas, and where employees can grow the culture and evolve it over time. So it's not me having a vision of 'This is our culture.' Maybe an analogy is, if you think of the employees and culture as plants growing, I'm not trying to be the biggest plant for them to aspire to. I'm more trying to architect the greenhouse where they can all flourish and grow."

"I believe that it's not about me," said Linda Heasley of The Limited. "I believe it's very much about the team. I believe that my associates can work anywhere they want, and my job is to re-recruit them every day and give them a reason to choose to work for us and for me as opposed to anybody else. So it's about making it fun. It's about making it exciting. It's about keeping them marketable. I encourage people: 'Go out and find out what the market bears. You should do that and then come back and help me figure out what you need in your development that you're not getting, because we owe you that.' I've been told by my associates that that's a countercultural approach to leadership: 'You're telling me to go look for another job?' But my point is that I should be able to re-recruit them. I should be able to get them convinced that this is the best opportunity for them. That's my philosophy."

Clarence Otis of Darden Restaurants said that selflessness was at the core of his leadership philosophy.

"It's a lesson that I learned early on, and it kept getting reinforced and cemented over time with a number of different leaders," Otis said. "It's this notion that leaders think about others first. They think about the people who are on the team, trying to help them get the job done. They think about the people they're trying to do a job for. Your thoughts are always there first, and you think about what the appropriate response for whatever that audience is, and you think last about 'what does this mean for me?'

"The guy who reinforced that most would have been my predecessor here at Darden, Joe Lee. I was CFO at the time, but on September 11, 2001, after it became clear what had happened, we had an all-employee meeting, and Joe started to talk. One of the first things he said was, 'We are trying to understand where all our people are who are traveling.' The second thing he said was: 'We've got a lot of Muslim teammates, managers in our restaurants, employees in our restaurants, who are going to be under a lot of stress during this period. And so, we need to make sure we're attentive to that.' And that was pretty powerful. Of all the things you could focus on that morning, he thought about the people who were on the road and then our Muslim colleagues."

Jana Eggers of Spreadshirt described the payoff—a sense of team accomplishment—for what are often very lonely moments.

"I think a lot of people have the perception that being the CEO is awesome, because you're the boss," she said. "You know, I get told regularly, 'But you make the decisions.' I'll say, 'Uh, no. I have to inspire a team to make the right decisions every day.' That's not an easy thing, because you don't make all the decisions. Maybe when you're a twenty-person company, in general you do, but when you get anywhere above, I'd say, five people, you're not really making all the decisions.

"It is a very lonely job. You're constantly in between a board and an entire company, and you're caught between those two things on a regular basis. And I think that's the thing that brings most CEOs to their knees. You feel very alone. There are times when I'm sitting in the office in Leipzig at ten p.m., and I'm saying to myself, 'I don't even know who I could call about this issue.' And I feel alone and frustrated and tired and all of those things. And I get that, and I'm okay with it. I know that it's coming, and I expect it. It's all a series of ups and downs.

"But what I love about it, why I do it, is that I really enjoy getting teams to do things they didn't think they could do. I like the team thing. That's what I get excited about. And when I see them proud of themselves, that's really cool, because that means that we got them there faster than they thought they could get there, or we got them there better than they thought they could get there. That's exciting."

It was a theme echoed by George Barrett of Cardinal Health: "I think a leader has to be comfortable with having the weight on his shoulders," he said. "And that's not for everybody. It can be hard, and it's a different experience if you haven't had to experience this. That's not for everybody, but I like it because I don't feel like I'm alone. I wind up bringing the group together, and we own the weight. I love that part of it."

The Right Balance

So what would a seasoned CEO say to those one hundred smart, energetic vice presidents, all of them hungry for advancement, whom we met at the beginning of this book? Are the trade-offs and pressures of being the boss worth the handsome wages?

"It's such a demanding job," said Kasper Rorsted of Henkel,

who added that his best advice to someone on track to be a CEO someday would be to ask him first, "Do you really want the job?"

"On the outside, it looks very shiny," he said. "But there's a lot of hard work, and you get paid to do all the uncomfortable things. You don't get paid to go play golf in Savannah. Everybody can do that, but it's not just glamour. I'm not saying it's hardship, but you have to be able to, as a person, live with it."

Learning to lead is hard, too. There's never an end point, and it can take years of trial and error before people feel comfortable in the role, striking the right balance of being friendly, though not friends, with the people they manage, and learning how to be a boss without being bossy.

It is the kind of learning process that can take the better part of a decade, as it did for Niki Leondakis of Kimpton Hotels and Restaurants.

"As an entry-level manager, I experienced what a lot of people experience, which is being too friendly with the people you manage and learning the appropriate boundaries and distances around certain things," she said. "I think people fall into one of two camps. Very few people become a supervisor or a boss for the first time and know exactly where the right balance is. Both with myself and all the young managers I see, people seem to swing to one end of the pendulum or the other—overzealous with power or 'I'm everybody's friend, and I want them to like me, and if they like me maybe they'll do what I ask and then it'll be easier.'"

For Leondakis, as it is for a lot of managers, it took years to get the pendulum to stop swinging.

"It was frankly just a long road of mistakes and learning and watching and trials and tribulations, really, about managing people, counseling people, hiring people, letting people go, and learning through the actual process of doing all those things over and over again that there's a middle ground that makes sense.

"When I started advancing in my career, I swung the pendulum the other way. I was at a point where most of my peers were men and they tended to act and behave differently than I did and came across as tough-minded and more rigid, a little more authoritarian. I felt that to be successful I needed to do that, too, so I was acting a lot like what I thought successful leadership looked like. That was in the early eighties. For women in general at that time, we all thought that to be successful or to be considered equal, you tried to dress like men, act like men, and ensure people knew you were tough-minded and could make the tough calls and be decisive.

"So I was holding back on some of my leadership strengths— collaboration, inclusion, and building and creating teams. I was trying to be somebody I wasn't, until one day I had to do something disciplinary to someone I really liked and admired. Human resources got involved and they wanted me to let this person go. I said, 'That's not fair.' So the negotiation between myself and human resources resulted in a week's suspension without pay for this person. I was struggling with how to communicate with her what had happened, because I couldn't reconcile for myself what the words were going to be.

"The person I worked for at that time could see my struggle and said, 'You know what, Niki? Just tap in to who you are as a woman and relate to her with compassion, and you'll be able to do what you need to do. You can still do what you have to do, but you don't have to be a jerk about it.' And that was sort of an epiphany for me, because I thought that being tough-minded and decisive and all those qualities and traits that I thought I was supposed to exhibit, that men exhibited, meant that I couldn't show compassion. It was a different experience for me to relate to this person with compassion and accountability at the same time, and balance the two. And the fact that it was effective was a huge lesson for me. From that point on, I had an awareness that there was this balance I could strike with being myself, being compassionate and holding people accountable. These were not mutually exclusive."

It is this sense of balance that, ultimately, may be hardest for leaders to achieve. There is a jumble of seeming contradictions to be resolved. Effective leaders must care about people enough to get the best work out of them, yet they must keep a distance so that any difficult conversations are about performance.

"I have learned to be distant without really being distant," said Lisa Price of Carol's Daughter. "I'm very friendly with everybody, but before I would get so invested and if there was a transition for whatever reason, it would hurt me to lose that person. And that discomfort is very hard to deal with, and it doesn't really have a place in business. So I've found this interesting space within myself, where I can have these really great relationships and work closely with people but still have that distance. I feel like I'm in a place now where I can be close to you and collaborative with you, but I don't get as emotionally attached."

There are other balances to achieve. Be confident—because people want to follow a confident leader—but not overconfident. Have a sense of everything that is going on at the company, and what needs to be done, yet be present—a word that many CEOs used—when talking to employees so they don't get the impression you're distracted. Sometimes leadership is about having the right answer; other times it's about having the right question.

Can leadership be taught? It is a question that CEOs often pose to themselves. It is a good question, but it needs to be parsed a little more to be answered. If the question is, can leadership be taught by one person to another, or to a group, the answer is no.

There are just too many variables. The onus is really on the student, the person who is learning to lead. They can learn from their experiences, from good bosses and bad bosses, from colleagues and peers, and from the stories told by other executives. All of these become pieces of a leadership puzzle that each of us has to put together for ourselves, in a way that makes sense, and in a way that works. Leaders who have solved the puzzle in their own way—at least to a point, since it is never quite finished—will convey authenticity. And it is authenticity that will be most effective in marshaling teams to work together to achieve a shared goal.

ACKNOWLEDGMENTS

I could not have written this book without the candid and wise insights from the dozens of leaders I interviewed over more than a year. Their contributions were invaluable.

Larry Ingrassia, the business editor of the *New York Times*, and Tim O'Brien, the editor of the Sunday Business section, were early and enthusiastic supporters of my interest in starting a weekly Q&A feature with CEOs about leadership, which became the basis for this book. Jim Collins, the author of *Good to Great, Built to Last*, and other influential books on leadership, offered smart suggestions for the list of open-ended questions that I've used for each of the interviews. I've worked for Rick Berke on the *Times*'s national desk since early 2010. He's been encouraging of this project at every step and embodies many of the leadership skills in this book.

A team of steady and sure hands helped me at key points in

this project. Christy Fletcher, my agent, provided savvy suggestions in shaping the book. Alex Ward, the editorial director of book development at the *New York Times*, offered counsel and encouragement early on. And I was fortunate to work with the team at Times Books, particularly Paul Golob, the editorial director, who gave me wise guidance on the direction and contours of the book, and provided deft edits on the final manuscript.

I am lucky to have a journalist for a father. Clellen Bryant, a former editor at *Time* and *Reader's Digest*, was an enormous help with early drafts. My mother, Julie, was, as always, encouraging from the start. And my stepmother, Jill, provided eagle-eyed proofreading.

Last, but most important, thanks to my family. My daughters, Anna and Sophia, were encouraging and understanding as this book consumed many weekends, and they helped keep me energized when I was flagging after a long day of writing by making me double espressos and beating me at Guitar Hero. My wife, Jeanetta, was my partner in this adventure. I can't list all the roles she played in this project, because there are too many. But thanks to her especially for being my sounding board for ideas, for her ear for language, and for her constant love and support.

INDEX

ABOUT THE AUTHOR

ADAM BRYANT is the deputy national editor of the *New York Times* and writes the popular "Corner Office" feature in the paper's Sunday Business section. He was the lead editor for the team that won the 2010 Pulitzer Prize for national reporting and is a former senior writer and business editor at *Newsweek*. He lives with his family in Westchester County, New York.